—American War Series—

THE MEXICAN WAR

"Mr. Polk's War"

Charles W. Carey, Jr.

 Enslow Publishers, Inc.
40 Industrial Road   PO Box 38
Box 398   Aldershot
Berkeley Heights, NJ 07922 Hants GU12 6BP
USA   UK
http://www.enslow.com

Let it be understood, then that we are not called upon to decide between a federalist and some other "ist," but to vote for or against Mr. Polk's war— for conquest and slavery.

—Excerpt from the *Portsmouth Journal of Literature and Politics,* June 26, 1847

Library of Congress Cataloging-in-Publication Data

Carey, Charles W.
    The Mexican War : "Mr. Polk's war" / Charles W. Carey, Jr.
       p. cm. — (American war series)
    Includes bibliographical references and index.
    ISBN 0-7660-1853-9
    1. Mexican War, 1846–1848—Juvenile literature. [1. Mexican War, 1846–1848.] I. Title. II. Series.
    E404 .C26   2002
    973.6'2—dc21
                           2001000817

Printed in the United States of America

10 9 8 7 6 5 4 3 2 1

To Our Readers:
We have done our best to make sure all Internet addresses in this book were active and appropriate when we went to press. However, the author and the publisher have no control over and assume no liability for the material available on those Internet sites or on other Web sites they may link to. Any comments or suggestions can be sent by e-mail to comments@enslow.com or to the address on the back cover.

Illustration Credits: Dover Publications, Inc., pp. 17, 24, 27, 54, 69; Enslow Publishers, Inc., pp. 14, 32, 76, 100, 110, 113, 116; Library of Congress, pp. 10, 20, 21, 23, 33, 42, 47, 50, 65, 74, 78, 89, 95; National Archives, p. 115; University of Texas at Austin, Special Collections Libraries, Benson Latin American Collection, pp. 38, 57, 60, 87.

Cover Illustration: Reproduced from the Collections of the Library of Congress.

Contents

Foreword

Letter from Anson Jones, President of the Republic of Texas, to James K. Polk, President of the United States, conveying Texas' approval of U.S. annexation terms.

Washington, on the Brazos, July 12, 1845.
To his Excellency James K. Polk, Etc. Etc. Etc.
Sir.

I avail myself with much pleasure of the opportunity afforded me by the return of General Besancon to address your Excellency this letter, and to communicate to you the gratifying intelligence, that the Deputies of the People of Texas assembled in Convention at the City of Austin on the 4th. Instant, and adopted on that day an ordinance expressing the acceptance and assent of the people to the proposal made by the government of the United States on the subject of the Annexation of Texas to the American Union.

This assent, given with promptness and with much unanimity, affords the assurance that this great measure, to the success of which, your Excellency is so sincerely attached, will be consummated without further difficulty and as I ardently hope in peace.

I shall have the further satisfaction to transmit to you very soon by request of the Convention, a copy of the ordinance I have now reference to, which will be placed in your hands by Mr. D. S. Kaufman, whom I have caused to be accredited as Charge d'Affaires of Texas near your Government, and I beg you to accept in the mean-time, assurances of the high regard with which I am

Your Excellency's Most Obedient and very humble servant
ANSON JONES

—from Steven R. Butler, ed., *A Documentary History of the Mexican War*
(Richardson, Texas: Descendants of Mexican War Veterans, 1995), p. 10

I heartily accept the motto,—"That government is best which governs least,"...Witness the present Mexican wars, the work of comparatively a few individuals using the standing government as their tool; for, in the outset, the people would not have consented to this measure.

—Henry David Thoreau in his book *Civil Disobedience*, 1848

1 The Battle of Chapultepec

 As they woke on the morning of September 13, 1847, three very different groups of young men knew that it might be their last day on earth. The enlisted men of Company E, 2nd Pennsylvania Infantry, United States Army, were getting ready to attack the Castle of Chapultepec, the most imposing fortress they had seen in Mexico. The Mexican cadets of the *Colegio Militar* (Military College) were getting ready to defend the castle against what promised to be the fiercest attack of the Mexican War. Meanwhile, the soldiers of the San Patricio Battalion, a Mexican unit captured by the Americans that was sentenced to die as soon as the Americans captured the castle, watched while the two

sides prepared to fight, hoping that somehow the Mexicans would win the battle and set them free.

Company E hailed from Westmoreland County, Pennsylvania. Most of its members were in their late teens and early twenties. They had volunteered to fight in Mexico, thinking the war would be a quick victory for the Americans. They wanted to earn glory and honor for themselves so they could return home as heroes. But after many months of hunger, thirst, sickness, filth, and fighting against Mexicans who usually outnumbered them, they were sick of war. And they now had to help capture the Castle of Chapultepec.[1]

Storming the Castle

The castle was a tall fortress that sat atop a steep hill on the outskirts of Mexico City. Climbing the hill with a heavy musket and a pack full of ammunition would be tough enough for the men of Company E even if the castle's defenders did not shoot at them. Getting inside the high, thick walls would be even tougher. There were only two ways the Americans could force their way in—knock down the front gate or climb over the walls on long, shaky scaling ladders. Neither one would be easy. The men of Company E knew there was a very good chance they would not survive the battle.

Although Chapultepec Castle looked very difficult to capture from the ground below, it was actually so small that it could hold only two hundred fifty defenders inside. About fifty of its defenders were cadets of the Colegio Militar, the Mexican military academy.

The Colegio Militar was housed in the castle. The cadets were a little younger than the men of Company E, mostly in their mid- to late teens. Nicholas Bravo, the Mexican Army general who had taken command of the castle with about two hundred troops, ordered the cadets to leave before the fighting began, but a few remained to fight. They knew that if the castle could hold out, then maybe the Americans would lose so many men that the brave Mexican Army could finally run them out of Mexico. And after all, they were training to be soldiers. What better training could there be than to fight in a real battle?[2]

Forty-six cadets joined their compatriots to defend the castle. The castle's defenders, including the cadets, fought bravely, but they were eventually overwhelmed by hundreds of Americans. According to legend, the cadets were among the last group of Mexican soldiers in the castle to stop fighting. During the battle, six cadets were killed—Fernando Montez de Oca, Juan de la Barrera, Francisco Márquez, Agustin Melgar, Juan Scutia, and Vicente Suárez Ferrer. Another three were wounded and thirty-seven were taken prisoner. Also according to legend, one of the cadets wrapped himself in the Mexican flag and hurled himself from the top of the wall into the mass of American troops down below. Another version of the legend has it that this cadet was waving the Mexican flag while running along the top of the wall when he was shot, and his body became wrapped in the flag as he fell to his death. Yet another version claims that all six cadets wrapped themselves in flags and jumped. The brave cadets became known as *Los Niños Héroes*, or the Heroic Children. They would long be remembered for their heroism in support of their nation.

Unlike the cadets of the Colegio Militar, most of the members of the San Patricio Battalion were not Mexicans. They were Irish immigrants who had joined the American Army and then deserted. The San Patricios were some of the bravest soldiers in the Mexican Army. They had fought courageously just a few days before at the Convent of San Mateo during the Battle of Churubusco on the outskirts of Mexico City. Despite their bravery, many of the San Patricios were captured at Churubusco and sentenced to death for being traitors. Thirty San Patricios were scheduled to be hanged as soon as the Castle of Chapultepec fell to the Americans.[3]

The Battle of Chapultepec

The Battle of Chapultepec began with an American artillery barrage (many cannons firing at the same target) against the castle. The Americans hoped the barrage would demoralize the Mexicans so much that they would surrender. The castle's defenders, however, were too determined. They would not give up without a fight to the finish.

The American infantry (foot soldiers) began its approach across open ground while the castle's guns fired on them. Company E marched to within three hundred yards of the castle and then charged. All around lay dead and wounded Americans who had attacked and fallen before them.

The men of Company E ran across a cornfield for about fifty yards, then came to a meadow of high tangled grass. Into the grass they ran while cannonballs fell all around them. In the meadow were seven or eight ditches, some of them ten to twelve feet wide. The ditches were filled with water about waist-deep and their bottoms were so muddy that in places the soldiers sank ankle-deep. Eventually, the men found a winding path that led through the grass and around the ditches. They followed the path to the base of the hill, where they collapsed, exhausted.

But the hardest part was still ahead. One officer ordered Company E to move out to the right while another ordered it to go to the left. In the confusion, the company's commander decided to ignore both orders. He led his men straight up the hill instead. By the time the men reached the main gate of the castle, some other American soldiers had already forced it open. Company E joined these soldiers and raced inside the castle walls.[4]

As Company E and other American soldiers began streaming into the castle, they were met by the Colegio Militar cadets and the other Mexican defenders in the castle courtyard. The courtyard was so small and the shooting so close that neither side had enough time to reload its weapons. After firing once, the soldiers either used their guns as clubs or attached bayonets to them and charged.

The fighting quickly degenerated into a chaotic free-for-all. As Thomas Barclay of Company E wrote, "everyone fights on his own hook."[5] The Mexican cadets fought bravely, jabbing and smashing the hated American invaders as best they could. But more and more Americans

The attack on the castle at Chapultepec was costly for the Americans, but it would ultimately win the war.

kept pouring into the castle, and the Mexican defenders, who had been few in number to begin with, were going down without being replaced. Eventually, the cadets and the other Mexican soldiers in the castle were so severely outnumbered that they were forced to surrender.

While all this action was taking place, the thirty deserters of the San Patricio Battalion were watching anxiously. Their American captors kept them standing in the hot sun for over two hours while the battle for the castle raged. Even worse, they were forced to stand in wagons with hangman's nooses around their necks. All of them knew that as soon as the American flag appeared in victory above the walls of the castle, they would be hanged. The last thing they would see in this life would be Old Glory. Desperately they watched, hoping and praying that somehow the Mexicans would win the battle and then set them free. But their prayers went unanswered. As soon as the men of the 2nd Pennsylvania raised the American flag over the Castle of Chapultepec, thirty horses were whipped, thirty wagons jerked forward, and the thirty San Patricios were left to twist in the wind.[6]

. . . the only way to treat John Bull [England] *was to look him straight in the eye.*

—Excerpt from the diary of President James Polk, January 4, 1846

2 Origins of the Mexican War

The Mexican War was the third major war fought by the United States. In the first two wars, the American Revolution and the War of 1812, American troops had fought mostly in the United States to obtain and preserve American independence. In the Mexican War, American troops fought mostly on foreign soil to gain new territory for the United States. In the eyes of many people, especially most Mexicans, the Mexican War was a "Yankee invasion" (Mexicans generally refer to all Americans, regardless of where they live, as Yankees).[1]

What led the United States to go to war against Mexico? There were two reasons for the outbreak of the Mexican War, one long term and the other short term. The long-term reason was the idea of Manifest Destiny.

This belief, extremely popular in the nineteenth century, claimed that Americans had been chosen by God to rule all of the North American continent between the Atlantic and Pacific oceans and between the Great Lakes and the Rio Grande. The short-term reason was the United States' annexation (taking over) of Texas, which was still claimed by Mexico. Manifest Destiny led Americans into a war with Mexico, while the desire to regain Texas led Mexicans into a war with the United States.

The Louisiana Purchase

In the early days of the Republic, most Americans made their living by farming. This meant that the United States had to be big enough so that its people could have enough land to farm. For a while, Americans seemed content controlling the land east of the Mississippi River and between Canada and Florida. In 1800, most Americans still lived east of the Appalachian Mountains. Although Kentucky was largely settled, the rest of the land west of the Appalachians was mostly forest inhabited by American Indians. It seemed as if the United States owned enough land to take care of future population growth for a long time to come.[2]

American attitudes about expansion began to change in 1803 when the United States bought the Louisiana Territory from France. At first, President Thomas Jefferson wanted to buy the city of New Orleans, Louisiana, because it controlled the mouth of the Mississippi River. If the United States owned New Orleans, then farmers west of the Appalachians could

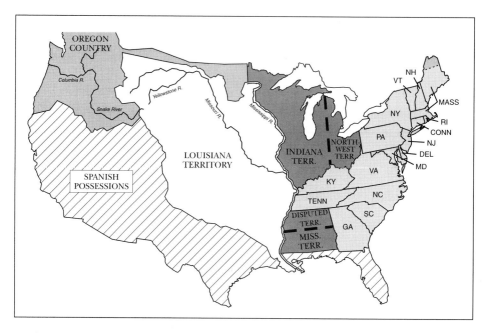

The Louisiana Purchase, which nearly doubled the territory of the United States, led Americans to dream of controlling all the land in North America from the Atlantic to the Pacific.

ship their goods to the eastern states by boat down the Ohio and Mississippi rivers to New Orleans, and from there up the east coast by ship. Although longer, this water route was faster and cheaper than hauling farm products by wagon over the roadless Appalachians. When the French offered to include all of their Louisiana lands between the Mississippi River and the Rocky Mountains as part of the New Orleans sale, Jefferson jumped at the chance, buying Louisiana for $15 million. As a result of the Louisiana Purchase, the United States nearly doubled in size, extending its borders two thirds of the way from the Atlantic Ocean to the Pacific Ocean.[3]

Not everyone was happy about the Louisiana Purchase. Some people thought the United States was big enough as it was and did not have a lot of money to throw away on "useless" land. But the Louisiana Purchase provided plenty of room for the American population to live as it grew bigger and bigger.

The War of 1812

Between 1803 and 1840, Americans took other steps to expand the borders of the United States. The War of 1812 was fought to keep the British from stopping American ships at sea as well as to get the British out of the Northwest Territory (present-day Ohio, Indiana, Illinois, Michigan, and Wisconsin), an area of rich farmland that the British had surrendered to the United States after the American Revolution but had never vacated. During the war, American troops invaded Canada in the hope of making it part of the United States, but the British Army drove them out. When the war ended in a stalemate, the British agreed to leave the Northwest Territory and the Americans agreed to leave Canada alone.

Further Expansion

From 1803 to 1819, Americans claimed that Texas, the northeast corner of New Spain (modern-day Mexico), was part of the Louisiana Purchase. The reason for this claim was that the boundaries of the Louisiana Territory were not well defined, mostly because very few people lived there. The Americans also wanted to take over Florida, another Spanish possession, because the Seminole

Indians who lived there often raided Americans living in Georgia. In 1819, the United States Army invaded Florida to crush these Indians. As a result, Spain offered Florida to the United States if the United States would give up its claim to Texas. The United States agreed.

For years, the United States had tried to gain control of Oregon Country (modern-day Oregon, Washington, and Idaho), another area of incredibly rich farmland. However, in 1818 it agreed to share Oregon Country with the British for twenty years after realizing that the British would not give up their claim to the territory without a fight.[4]

Manifest Destiny

Many Americans continued to believe that the United States should continue to expand its borders even further. After 1840, foreign immigration increased dramatically, which made the eastern states more crowded and encouraged more Americans to move to the lands west of the Mississippi River. In 1845, John L. O'Sullivan, the editor of *United States Magazine and Democratic Review*, spurred Americans to action by putting their feelings into powerful words. O'Sullivan wrote that it was America's "manifest destiny to overspread the continent allotted by Providence." He meant that he believed it was God's will that Americans should govern all of North America, including Canada and Mexico. A number of American politicians and newspaper editors echoed O'Sullivan's call to action. The phrase *Manifest Destiny* quickly became part of the American political language.[5]

President James Monroe set forth a strong position for the United States, warning Europe not to try to set up new colonies in the Western Hemisphere.

Manifest Destiny seemed to go hand in hand with the Monroe Doctrine. In December 1823, President James Monroe had proclaimed that the United States would not tolerate any European interference in the new nations of Central and South America that had just gained their independence from Spain. This meant that the United States saw itself as the power in charge of both North and South America.

Although most Americans believed in Manifest Destiny, few could agree on exactly which lands the United States was supposed to govern. Nor could they agree on whether those lands should be captured by

American troops or bought with American dollars. Some thought that the British should be driven out of Canada. Others urged that Mexico and Central America should become part of the United States. Some wanted to take over the Caribbean islands and South America, and some even talked about acquiring some of the Pacific islands, like Hawaii and Samoa, and parts of Asia. But just about everyone who believed in Manifest Destiny agreed that it meant annexing Texas, obtaining Oregon from the British, and obtaining California and New Mexico from the Mexicans. In 1844, Americans elected James K. Polk president, mostly because he promised to acquire Oregon and Texas for the United States.[6]

By 1847, the ownership of Oregon Country was settled. Although both the United States and Great Britain had threatened to go to war over Oregon, neither really wanted to, and so they agreed to split Oregon in two. The British kept the northern half (modern-day British Columbia) and the Americans kept the southern half (modern-day Oregon, Washington, Idaho, and parts of Montana and Wyoming).[7]

Obtaining California and New Mexico proved to be a harder task than obtaining Oregon.

The Struggle for Texas

After Mexico obtained its independence from Spain in 1821, the United States tried to buy Texas from the Mexicans. Instead of selling, the Mexicans invited private American citizens to settle in Texas. The Mexican government was concerned that Texas was not heavily populated enough to keep the United States from taking it by force. Only about thirty-five hundred Mexicans and an unknown number of Indians, mostly Apache and Comanche, lived in Texas at the time. The Mexicans believed that, if they could get more settlers to come to Texas, then the economy would improve and tax revenues would increase. They also hoped the new emigrants could be made into loyal citizens of Mexico, making the Americans think twice before they tried to take the territory. So in 1824, Mexico offered cheap land and low taxes to any American who would settle in Texas. Of course, new settlers had to pledge allegiance to Mexico, they had to become Roman Catholic (the official religion of Mexico), and they had to promise to give up slavery.[8]

At first, the plan seemed to work. Over the next six years, seven thousand Americans settled in Texas, including Stephen Austin, Sam Houston, and Jim Bowie, who would become famous for their adventures in Texas. Most of them came to plant cotton and other crops, and the Texas economy began to boom.

The Mexican government, however, eventually realized that most Americans in Texas were still loyal to the United States and had never really given up their own religious beliefs. Many of these American settlers also insisted on owning slaves, which was illegal in Mexico. Alarmed by these developments, in 1830, Mexico banned any more Americans from settling in Texas. By now, however, it was too late. Over the next five years, Americans continued to settle in Texas. By 1835, the American population in Texas was over twenty thousand.[9]

In 1835, the Mexican government tried to tighten its authority over Texas. But the Texans resisted, and in 1836, they declared their independence from Mexico. At first, it seemed that the Mexican government would easily crush the revolt. The president of Mexico, General Antonio López de Santa Anna, personally led an army of six thousand men into Texas. At the Battle of the Alamo, an old Spanish mission in San Antonio, the Mexicans completely wiped out the Alamo's 183 defenders,

Stephen Austin is known as the Father of Texas for his efforts to bring American colonists to the territory.

although the badly outnumbered Americans put up a spirited fight that lasted for days. Among those killed were the famous frontiersmen Davy Crockett and Jim Bowie. Then, at the Battle of Goliad, the Mexicans massacred three hundred fifty Texans rather than take them prisoner. These defeats, however, gave the American forces under Sam Houston time to organize a response. At the Battle of San Jacinto, the Texans were able to turn the tables on the Mexicans. According to legend, Sam

The Mexican Army killed all the Texans who defended the Alamo in the war for Texan independence. However, the battle gave Sam Houston time to gather his troops before facing Santa Anna.

Houston's army of eight hundred men caught the Mexicans taking a siesta (a midday nap) and slaughtered most of them before they were up and ready to fight. They even managed to capture General Santa Anna, and forced him to sign a treaty granting Texas its independence. Although the Mexican government rejected the treaty, it never sent another army into Texas.[10]

The Issue of Annexation

In 1836, Texas, now calling itself the independent Republic of Texas, applied for admission as a state to the United States. For nine years, Congress debated the wisdom of annexing Texas. At first, the Senate was reluctant to admit Texas, partly because it feared a war with Mexico, so the application was rejected. As time went on, however, war with Mexico seemed less likely, considering the fact that the Mexicans had never tried to recapture Texas even though they still claimed it. Many Americans now feared that an independent Texas would acquire New Mexico and California before the United States could do so.

As a result, the annexation of Texas became the most important issue of the election of 1844. Campaigning on a platform that strongly supported Manifest Destiny goals, Democrat James K. Polk was elected president. Polk and the Democrats favored annexation, so in 1845, Congress voted to make Texas a state. However, Mexico, which still claimed Texas, protested the annexation by breaking off diplomatic relations with the United States.[11]

The Battle of San Jacinto, in which Texans under the command of Sam Houston defeated Mexican troops under Santa Anna, marked the end of the war for Texan independence.

In 1845, Polk made James Slidell a "Minister Extraordinary and Plenipotentiary" and sent him to Mexico City to offer the Mexicans $30 million for California and New Mexico. However, the Mexicans were still upset over the annexation of Texas and they refused to even listen to Slidell's offer. Instead, they promised to take back Texas.[12]

American greed for Texas was partly to blame for the outbreak of the Mexican War. However, Mexico's inability to control Texas also played a large part in bringing about the war.

The immediate cause of war between the United States and Mexico was a border dispute between the two

countries. Texans claimed that the Rio Grande, a river
that flows into the Gulf of Mexico near Matamoros, was
the border between Texas and Mexico. Mexicans, on the
other hand, claimed the Nueces River, which flows into
the Gulf of Mexico at Corpus Christi, about two hundred
miles to the north of Matamoros, as the border. The area
between the two rivers contained much of what the
Mexicans considered New Mexico, but neither Mexico
nor Texas pressed its claim as long as Texas remained an
independent country.

After the annexation of Texas in 1845, the United
States insisted that Mexico observe the Rio Grande as the
border. In January 1846, Polk ordered General Zachary

James Polk became president through a campaign supporting
Manifest Destiny. When he took office, he set out to win territory
for the United States—even if it meant going to war with Mexico.

Taylor to take four thousand men—at that time half of the entire United States Army—and occupy a position on the Rio Grande near Matamoros, where three thousand Mexican troops were stationed.

For three months, both sides eyed each other cautiously. Shooting broke out in April when an eleven-man American patrol looking for a missing officer was ambushed and wiped out. A few days later, another American patrol was ambushed. This time, sixty-three men were killed, wounded, or captured.

This incident gave Polk just what he needed. On May 11, 1846, Polk asked Congress for a declaration of war against Mexico, claiming that the Mexicans had "shed the blood of our fellow-citizens on our own soil."[13] Not all congressmen were convinced of the truth of Polk's claim. Abraham Lincoln, who had just been elected to the House of Representatives from Illinois, asked to be shown the exact spot on which American blood had been shed. Several others thought Polk was using a minor incident as an excuse to seize Mexican territory. But most congressmen were in favor of war—and the chance to win new territory for the United States. The day after Polk's request, both the House and the Senate voted to declare war against Mexico.[14]

By 1846, the American belief in Manifest Destiny had made the United States willing to fight for California and New Mexico. But American efforts to make Manifest Destiny come true had also made the Mexicans willing to fight to regain Texas.

As war exists, and, notwithstanding all our efforts to avoid it, exists by the act of Mexico herself, we are called upon by every consideration of duty and patriotism to vindicate with decision the honor, the rights, and the interests of our country.

—Special message of President James Polk asking Congress to declare war with Mexico on May 11, 1846

3 From Fort Texas to Monterrey

Between April and September 1846, the United States Army under General Zachary Taylor defeated the Mexican Army in three major battles without a loss and effectively occupied northeastern Mexico. However, its victories were not decisive enough to force the Mexicans to give up. By late September, the Americans realized that many difficulties faced Taylor's army if it continued marching on Mexico City, the Mexican capital. These difficulties forced President James K. Polk and General Winfield Scott, General-in-Chief of the United States Army, to abandon their original strategy of marching on the Mexican capital from the north. Instead, they would have to come up with a new strategy for winning the war.

Taylor on the Defensive

Zachary Taylor was not the typical American general. He hated to wear his dress uniform and preferred to dress in old, beat-up clothes. Many visitors to his headquarters mistook him for an orderly. One young lieutenant, who obviously did not know what the general looked like, even offered him a dollar to clean his sword! But Taylor's men loved him because he was one of the few officers willing to share in their suffering. If they went hungry or thirsty or slept out in the open, then so did he. Because of all this, Taylor's men affectionately nicknamed him "Old Rough and Ready."[1]

General Zachary Taylor, known as "Old Rough and Ready," took command of the American forces in the Mexican War.

The first order of business for the Army of Occupation, as Taylor's army was called, was to occupy the disputed territory between the Rio Grande and Nueces rivers. After leaving Corpus Christi in late March, Taylor's army marched south without meeting any Mexican resistance. They established a supply base at Point Isabel, just north of the Rio Grande on the Gulf of Mexico. Taylor then concentrated most of his forces at Fort Texas (later renamed Fort Brown), just across the river from Matamoros where three thousand Mexican troops under the command of General Pedro de Ampudia were stationed.

Ampudia was greatly feared by his men. He had a reputation for being cruel. In 1844, after ordering the execution of a prisoner named Francisco Sentmanat, Ampudia had Sentmanat's head fried in oil so it would last longer on public display.

From Fort Texas and Point Isabel, the Americans could easily control the disputed area between the two rivers. But in late April, Matamoros was reinforced by an additional three thousand Mexican troops. The entire command of the Mexican Army of the North (so called because it fought in the north part of Mexico) was given to General Mariano Arista, one of the Mexican Army's most popular leaders. Unlike Ampudia, Arista had a reputation for being one of the Mexican Army's best generals and for treating his troops fairly. Suddenly, Taylor's Army of Occupation found itself outnumbered six thousand to four thousand and facing a force commanded by a popular, competent general.[2]

Arista lost little time in attempting to take advantage of his superior numbers. On May 1, he crossed the Rio Grande to the east of Fort Texas with the main body of his army. At the same time, he sent the rest of his men to cross the river to the north. Arista planned to outflank the Americans and either surround or destroy them. He hoped to capture at least the supplies at Point Isabel, which was not well defended, and starve the Americans into surrender.[3]

The United States Has Its Advantages

Though they were outnumbered, the Americans had three important advantages. First, all of Taylor's troops were trained professionals. These men had volunteered for military service because they wanted to make the army their career. They had been drilled and disciplined for many months. They were equipped with modern firearms, durable uniforms, and high-quality leather boots. They were fed wholesome food (although much of it was not very tasty), they had plenty of water to drink, and they were provided with decent medical care. In addition, as citizens who had a right to vote, many felt they had a personal stake in a war that affected their country's future. Most of the Mexican troops, on the other hand, were Indians and peasants who had little training as soldiers. The Mexican infantry was equipped mostly with hand-me-down muskets bought cheaply from the British Army, and the Mexican Army did not always have enough ammunition or gunpowder. Many soldiers wore civilian clothes—usually a faded sombrero, an old poncho, and a worn pair of breeches. Some wore sandals instead of boots. They often had to scrounge for food and water, and they rarely received medical treatment. In addition, they had no role in Mexican politics, so their willingness to fight for their country was low. In fact, the only reason many of them were serving in the army at all was because they had been forced to become soldiers by the Mexican government.[4]

The Americans' second advantage was that the United States Army artillery corps was one of the world's best. American artillerymen were trained to fire rapidly and accurately. Their biggest guns were twenty-four-pounders (guns that fired a cannonball or shell weighing twenty-four pounds), which were accurate at ranges up to a mile. The Americans also had a number of light artillery batteries that used six- and twelve-pounders. These guns were so light that they could be limbered (attached to horses for transport) quickly and hauled within minutes to wherever they were needed on the battlefield. They could then be unlimbered just as rapidly and used to support an attack on a weak enemy position or to defend against a strong enemy attack. These batteries could travel so fast that they seemed to fly across the battlefield, and so they were often called "flying artillery."[5] They would be up against the Mexican artillery corps—one of the world's worst. Its artillerymen were not well trained, its biggest guns were eighteen-pounders with a range much shorter than the American guns, and it had no flying artillery.

The United States' third advantage was its naval forces. The United States Navy was far superior to the Mexican Navy. American ships were faster, more numerous, and better armed than Mexican ships. In no time, the United States Navy's Home Squadron blockaded the entire Gulf Coast of Mexico. This meant that General Taylor's army could be supplied and reinforced by sea at its base at Point Isabel rather than by long overland supply lines that could be easily attacked. It also meant that the Mexican Army, which was poorly supplied to begin with, could not receive any additional weapons or supplies from overseas.

Throughout the war, the Home Squadron played a small but important role. Supplies for the American Army were delivered quickly and efficiently by merchant ships under the squadron's protection. In addition to blockading the major Mexican Gulf ports of Matamoros, Tampico, and Veracruz, the squadron also landed marines at a number of smaller harbors to prevent small ships from landing supplies for the Mexicans. Early in the war, the squadron operated entirely out of New Orleans, Louisiana. When this port proved to be too far away to support all the squadron's activities, the squadron captured Tampico, Mexico, and used it as an advance base.

Despite these American advantages, Arista's Mexican Army—which planned to trap the Americans between Matamoros and Point Isabel—alarmed Taylor. On May 1, he shifted most of his troops out of Fort Texas to Point Isabel. Fortunately for Taylor, the Mexicans moved too slowly to get between his army and Point Isabel, so their

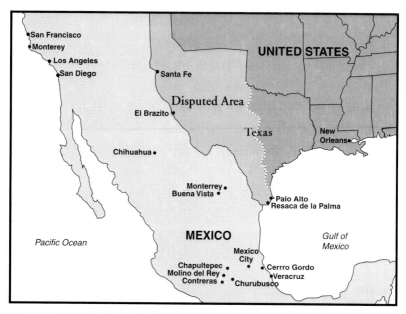

Mexico, as it looked at the time the American forces under General Taylor began their campaign.

trap failed. Arista then besieged (surrounded and attacked) Fort Texas while the main body of his army pursued Taylor, but the fort was too strong and its defenders were too determined.[6]

The Battle of Palo Alto

After strengthening the defenses at Point Isabel, Taylor began marching his army back to Fort Texas to break the Mexican siege. Meanwhile, Arista's main body continued to advance slowly toward Point Isabel. On May 8, the two armies collided at Palo Alto, about halfway between Point Isabel and Matamoros.

Arista wisely chose to block the road to Matamoros. This meant that the outnumbered Americans would have to attack, which he knew usually resulted in greater casualties than defending. Arista positioned his infantry on flat ground between a swamp and a wooded hill where it could not be outflanked. Then he positioned his cavalry on the sides of the infantry so the horsemen could surround the American infantry as it advanced. Between the Mexican and American lines was a big field of tall grass and chaparral (scrub brush), which made it hard for Taylor to see and control his troops while they attacked. From the Mexican standpoint, it was an excellent defensive position that would not be easy to attack.

Rather than face the overwhelming odds against him, Taylor decided not to attack. Instead, he set up his

General Zachary Taylor and the United States Army fought General Mariano Arista at Palo Alto. This battle began a long struggle for control over western lands.

long-range artillery just out of range of the Mexican artillery and opened up a deadly fire on the Mexican ranks. As his men began falling, Arista realized that it was now he, not Taylor, who would have to either attack or retreat. Since the chaparral prevented an infantry attack, Arista ordered a cavalry charge on the American right side. This attack was easily repulsed by American infantry and flying artillery, so Arista ordered another cavalry attack, this time on the American left flank. This charge was repulsed, too.

At this point in the battle, a wad from an American artillery shell set the grass on fire, creating so much smoke that neither side could see the other. Under cover of smoke, both armies changed their positions. But after another two hours of artillery fire, Arista ran out of ammunition and ordered his men to withdraw beyond artillery range. The Battle of Palo Alto, during which five hundred Mexicans and four Americans were killed, had come to an end. The Americans could claim victory, but Arista's army had only been bruised—not destroyed. Despite its losses, Arista's forces were still larger than the American Army.

The Battle of Resaca de la Palma

On the morning after the Battle of Palo Alto, Arista's army took up a new defensive position about five miles from Matamoros at a place called Resaca de la Palma. Here, the road to Matamoros ran through a *resaca,* a shallow ravine where the Rio Grande used to flow. Once again, Arista blocked the road. This time, he formed his lines on both sides of the resaca in chaparral that was even taller and thicker than what they had faced at Palo Alto. He also positioned his artillery so that it commanded the road as it ran through the resaca. Once again, Arista had chosen an excellent defensive position.[7]

The chaparral hid the Mexicans from the American gunners, so a repeat performance of the day before was impossible. This time, Taylor decided to plow through the middle of the Mexican defenses by charging his four infantry regiments straight down the road. But before this plan could work, the Mexican artillery commanding the road would have to be silenced.

A battery of flying artillery was sent to do the job. But before it could force the Mexican artillerymen to abandon their position, it was attacked by Mexican cavalry and had to retreat.

Next, Taylor sent a company of dragoons (mounted riflemen) to silence the Mexican artillery. The dragoons charged so hard that they ran through and past the guns, which temporarily put the Mexican artillery out of action. But then the dragoons were attacked by Mexican infantry. They, too, were forced to retreat. Finally, the 5th and 8th Infantry Regiments were sent to capture the Mexican guns. After several minutes of savage fighting, they succeeded. Almost immediately, they were attacked by more Mexican cavalry, but the Americans were able to defend themselves without having to retreat. Then the 8th Infantry charged across the resaca and cleared the road of Mexican troops. This opened the way for the rest of Taylor's army to race down the road and cut the Mexican forces in two.

The American attack could have been repelled easily if the Mexicans had been working together as a team. However, they were spread out so far along both sides of the resaca that most of the Mexican soldiers could only watch the battle, not take part in it. Arista thought the fighting over the Mexican guns was a diversion, so he kept his troops in their positions and never ordered an attack. By the time Arista realized what was happening, the center of his defenses had been overrun by Americans and his entire army was retreating helter-skelter. Most of the Mexicans did not stop running until they had crossed the Rio Grande into Matamoros.[8]

The Battle of Resaca de la Palma was a major victory for the Americans. Their casualties totalled forty-nine killed and about eighty-three wounded. Mexican casualties were estimated at seven hundred killed and wounded in battle, three hundred drowned while crossing the Rio Grande, and more than one thousand deserters.[9]

Taylor Marches on Monterrey

For eight days, the two armies stared at each other across the Rio Grande. During this time, Arista tried to regroup his shattered army while Taylor made plans to attack Matamoros. On May 17, the Americans crossed the river in force. To their surprise, they discovered that the Mexican Army had abandoned the city the night before. The Mexicans were retreating south to Monterrey, the capital of the Mexican state of Nuevo Leon and the most important city in northeastern Mexico. Taylor then began making plans to attack Monterrey.[10]

After his victory at Resaca de la Palma, Taylor had to figure out what to do with the thousands of American volunteers who were now arriving at his camp. These volunteers had enlisted for ninety days and were organized into state regiments commanded by civilian officers. For the most part, these volunteer units lacked training and discipline. Worst of all, Taylor lacked the necessary food, drinking water, tents, and medical supplies to maintain them. It took Taylor over two months to outfit and organize the volunteers properly for the advance on Monterrey.

During these months, the volunteers got a good taste of the realities of war. They had left home dreaming of becoming war heroes. Now they found themselves hanging around the American camp with nothing to do, not enough to eat or drink, and too little shelter from the hot days and cold nights of northern Mexico. One of the army camps was located next to a swamp, and the soldiers were constantly bothered by mosquitoes and mud. Other camps had it better. There, the men had only to deal with snakes, scorpions, spiders, and lots and lots of ants. Because food and shelter were scarce and the men were bored, they fought with each other like children. One of the biggest camp battles took place when a regiment from Ohio accused a regiment from Maryland of stealing a catfish. Sadly, during these two months fifteen hundred volunteers—far more than were killed by the Mexicans in battle—died from disease and exposure to the elements without ever seeing action against the enemy. Of those who survived, many either deserted or simply returned home after their ninety-day enlistment expired.[11]

Meanwhile, major changes were taking place in the Mexican Army of the North. By the time Arista reached Monterrey, his army had dwindled to about one thousand infantry and a few detachments of cavalry. Disgusted by Arista's loss at Resaca de la Palma, Mexican President Mariano Paredes replaced him, first with General Tomas Mejia and then a short while later with General Pedro de Ampudia. Ampudia had been replaced by Arista at Matamoros, so this was a second chance for Ampudia to prove himself a hero. While these appointments were made, the Army of the North was reinforced several times. By September, Ampudia had almost ten thousand men.[12]

From late July to mid-August, the American Army of Occupation moved up the Rio Grande to Camargo,

Mexican General Arista was replaced after his defeat at the Battle of Resaca de la Palma.

about one hundred miles northeast of Monterrey. Here, Taylor realized how difficult it would be to cross the desert between Camargo and Monterrey with all his men and supplies. So he decided to take only three thousand of the seventy-seven hundred volunteers (he picked the ones who were properly disciplined and equipped) as well as the remaining thirty-two hundred regulars, for a total force of sixty-two hundred. Once again, the Army of Occupation would be outnumbered by the Army of the North.

Taylor's men met little resistance until they reached the northern outskirts of Monterrey on September 19. They quickly realized that taking the city would not be as easy as reaching it had been. The north side of Monterrey was protected by the Citadel, a dark, castlelike fortress that the Americans called the Black Fort. The east side was defended by El Tenería, an old tannery building whose walls had been reinforced, and El Diablo (the Devil's Fort), which was made of stone. The west side was guarded by the Bishop's Palace on the Mountain of Obispado (also known as Independence Hill) and El Soldado (The Soldier) on Federacion Hill. The south side was protected by the Santa Catarina River and the Sierra Madre mountains. And many of the buildings in Monterrey were made of stone, making the entire city one huge fortress. Monterrey would be a very tough nut for the Americans to crack. But if the Americans hoped to continue on to Mexico City, they were going to have to find a way to crack it.

I declare to the inhabitants of California, that although I come in arms with a powerful force, I do not come among them as an enemy of California; on the contrary, I come as their best friend—as henceforward California will be a portion of the United States . . .

—John D. Sloat, commander of the United States Navy's Pacific Squadron, Harbor of Monterey, July 7, 1846

4 From Missouri to California

 While General Zachary Taylor's army invaded northeastern Mexico, the much smaller Army of the West was campaigning in New Mexico and Upper California. The territory that Taylor's army captured never became part of the United States, but the western lands that the Army of the West conquered did. Even though this group of American soldiers was small, in the long run its accomplishments would actually be more important to the United States than those of Taylor's army.

New Mexico

When the Spanish settled there in 1598, New Mexico was home to perhaps twenty-five thousand American

Indians, mostly Pueblo. Over the next two hundred fifty years, the Hispanic residents mixed with the Pueblo and built a local economy based on cattle and sheep ranching. The large estates where this ranching took place were located mostly along the Rio Grande, especially near the small towns of Albuquerque and Taos, and around the capital at Santa Fe. A prosperous trade between Santa Fe and Independence, Missouri, was conducted along the Santa Fe Trail by a handful of American traders operating out of Santa Fe. However, few people other than Pueblo, Apache, and Navajo Indians lived in the rest of New Mexico. It was mostly desert and mountains.[1]

In 1846, New Mexico's population consisted of slightly more than fifty thousand Mexicans, perhaps thirty thousand Indians, and approximately one thousand Americans. These people felt little attachment to the rest of Mexico, partly because their commercial ties were stronger with the United States, and partly because the Mexican government paid little attention to them. The result was a New Mexican society that felt little loyalty to the federal government in Mexico City over one thousand miles away.[2]

The American merchants in Santa Fe wanted New Mexico to join the United States so they could avoid Mexican trade regulations. They also hoped they would have more control over local affairs than they did under Mexican rule. Also, a growing number of Americans from east of the Mississippi River wanted to relocate to California. The overland trail that ran through New Mexico stayed open year-round, while trails to the north of New Mexico were impassable during the winter. In addition, Texans claimed the section of New Mexico east of the Rio Grande as part of their state. For these reasons, Americans wanted New Mexico for themselves.

Kearny Takes New Mexico

On May 13, 1846, the same day Congress declared war against Mexico, President James K. Polk ordered Colonel Stephen W. Kearny to conquer New Mexico. Kearny was commander of the 1st Dragoons Regiment. Kearny was an excellent choice to lead this expedition. He had

Colonel Stephen Kearny headed a small army to take control of New Mexico and California and gain more territory for the United States.

spent the last thirty years as an army officer in the West. He probably knew more about the lay of the land and understood American Indians better than any other officer in the United States Army. He also had a reputation for being tough but fair and for being an excellent leader when the going got tough.

In addition to the three hundred dragoons, Kearny's force included a volunteer unit, the 1st Missouri Mounted Infantry Regiment under Colonel Alexander W. Doniphan, and three batteries of artillery. The Army of the West, as Kearny's force was called, totaled sixteen hundred men.

The Army of the West left Independence, Missouri, in late June 1846. Although the troops followed the Santa Fe Trail almost the entire way, the trip was not easy. It was summer, so the men could not find enough grass along the way to feed their hungry animals or enough water to drink. At least sixty horses died during the journey. Fortunately, all the men survived. Kearny's troops finally reached New Mexico in August, after traveling nine hundred hot and exhausting miles.

Meanwhile, the Mexican governor of New Mexico, Manuel Armijo, found out that Kearny's army was approaching. Five years earlier, Armijo had easily defeated a band of almost three hundred Texas volunteers who had come to stake the Republic of Texas's claim over New Mexico. This experience made him confident that he could defeat Kearny's men, too. But when Armijo tried to raise a defensive force, he discovered that very few New Mexicans were willing to fight for Mexico against the

United States. He then appealed urgently for help to the Mexican military outpost in Chihuahua several hundred miles to the south, but none was sent. When Kearny's men showed up on the outskirts of Santa Fe in mid-August, Armijo had fled to Albuquerque. The locals he left behind offered no resistance to the American forces. The battle for New Mexico was over before it started.

California

Kearny's orders called for him to continue on to California if he thought he could make the trip before winter came. He left behind some men in case the New Mexicans tried to revolt, and he sent the Missouri volunteers and about half of the dragoons south to join General Zachary Taylor's army at Monterrey. Then Kearny and the rest of the Army of the West set out for the Pacific Ocean.

In many respects, California Territory (modern-day California, Arizona, Nevada, and Utah, as well as parts of Colorado and Wyoming) was like New Mexico. Its economy revolved around cattle ranching, and its residents lived mostly in one place—in what is modern-day California. In addition to the small coastal towns of Yerba Buena (modern-day San Francisco), Monterey, San Pedro, San Diego, and Los Angeles (the territorial capital), a number of people lived on big ranches in the Sacramento Valley. Trade flourished between these communities and the United States via the Overland Trail, which ran from California to Santa Fe, where it connected with the Santa Fe Trail. The rest of the territory was inhabited by American Indians, fur trappers, and miners.[3]

In 1846, California's entire population was slightly more than twenty-five thousand. This total included about fifteen thousand American Indians from a number of tribes as well as approximately ten thousand Californios, the Mexican descendents of the Spanish settlers of the area. California also contained about twelve hundred whites of non-Hispanic descent, including about eight hundred Americans.[4]

Politically and socially, the Californios were very much like New Mexicans. Their commercial ties were stronger with the United States than with Mexico, and the Mexican government took even less interest in what happened in California than in what happened in New Mexico. Mexico City was thousands of miles away, and the governor had little power because the state's settlements were so far apart. A dispute between Governor Pio Pico in Los Angeles and General Jose Maria Castro in Monterey further weakened the government. A series of revolutions in the 1840s had made the Mexican government's hold on California so weak, in fact, that the territory was now a semi-independent region. Few Californios felt any loyalty to the Mexican government.

Millions of acres of fertile land and the rumor that there was gold and silver in the Sacramento Valley made California an attractive place for Americans who wanted to go west. In 1835, President Andrew Jackson had tried to buy northern California, and in 1842, a United States Navy commodore misinterpreted his orders and temporarily seized the port of Monterey. Clearly, the United States was eager to acquire California and was looking for any excuse to do so.

Unlike the Mexicans in New Mexico, who did not seem to care if they belonged to Mexico or the United States, the Californios were a fiercely independent group. Most of the Americans living in California wanted it to join the United States, because it would make trade easier and because they hoped it would give them more influence over local affairs. But Californios opposed this idea. They feared statehood would bring in too many Americans, who would eventually take control of California away from the Californios. Unlike the New Mexicans, when American troops tried to take over California, the Californios would fight back.

The Struggle for California

By the time Kearny crossed the Colorado River into modern-day California in December, the struggle for California was well under way. In mid-June 1846, a group of about one hundred fifty American settlers in the Sacramento Valley formed the California Battalion. Their leader was John C. Frémont, a United States Army captain and surveyor who had been sent to California by the United States government to make maps—not to take it over. Like Kearny, Frémont was a veteran who had spent many years in the West. He commanded a great deal of respect from his men. After defeating a band of poorly organized Californio horsemen, Frémont's followers declared the independence of California from

Mexico. Because their flag had a picture of a grizzly bear on it, their "country" was also known as the Bear Flag Republic. However, rather than remain independent, the Republic wanted to join the United States as soon as possible.[5]

On July 2, Commodore John D. Sloat, commander of the United States Navy's Pacific Squadron, entered the harbor of Monterey, California, with five ships while on a routine cruise. When he heard about the creation of the Bear Flag Republic, he landed two hundred fifty marines and sailors and took control of Monterey. He also sent a

John C. Frémont, who led a government-backed expedition to explore parts of the American West, went to California, where he helped settlers there fight for independence from Mexico.

force to capture Yerba Buena. Now that they had the support of the United States military behind them, the men of the California Battalion put an end to the Bear Flag Republic and declared California a loyal territory of the United States.

On July 23, Sloat, who was old enough to retire from the military, was relieved by Commodore Robert F. Stockton. Stockton was an energetic veteran of the United States Navy and a man with a reputation for being quite resourceful when the occasion demanded. This was fortunate for the Americans, because the situation now demanded that Stockton take command of all the units—sea and land, regular and volunteer—fighting in California under the American flag.

Stockton immediately sent the California Battalion to capture San Diego from another Californio militia force and sent about three hundred marines and sailors to capture Los Angeles. This time, the Californios offered little resistance. By mid-August, all of California was in the hands of the American military.

However, the Californios had not given up. They were just waiting for the right moment to attack. That moment came when the California Battalion returned to the Sacramento Valley (where it stayed during the rest of the struggle for California) and Stockton returned to Monterey. Led by Captain José María Flores, in late September, three hundred Californios rose up and ran the Americans out of Los Angeles and San Diego. When an American force of four hundred marines and sailors tried to retake Los Angeles, Flores's men ran them off as well. By the time Kearny arrived in California in December, the Californios controlled the southern half and the Americans controlled the northern half.

On December 5, Kearny was joined by some of Stockton's men in the Valley of San Pasqual, in southeastern California just west of the Colorado River. The next day, Kearny's men ran into a large force of Californio cavalrymen blocking the way out of the valley. Although they were outnumbered and no longer had any horses, Kearny decided to attack. It was a bad decision. Some of the Californios pretended to retreat, and when Kearny's men chased them, the rest of the Californios surrounded and attacked the Americans. Eighteen Americans died and another thirteen were wounded in this encounter, known as the Battle of San Pasqual. The Californios suffered minimal casualties.

Kearny's men managed to retreat to a rocky hilltop. Once again, the Californios surrounded them. This time, however, the Americans' position was too difficult to attack. Instead, the Californios kept the Americans from leaving their hilltop to look for food and water. After five days, Kearny's men were desperately hungry and thirsty. They were getting ready to attempt a breakout attack when a large force of American marines and sailors under Stockton's command miraculously arrived and saved Kearny's men.[6]

Kearny's men continued their long march until they reached San Diego, which Stockton's men had already recaptured. For three weeks, Kearny's exhausted dragoons rested while he drilled the sailors until they made respectable soldiers. Then the three-hundred-man Army of the West, this time under the command of Stockton, marched on Los Angeles. On January 8, 1847, four hundred fifty mounted Californios attacked the Americans twelve miles from Los Angeles at the San Gabriel River. The American infantry easily repulsed several cavalry charges with the help of the artillery, and eventually, the Californios were forced to retreat. This action, known as the Battle of San Gabriel, resulted in fourteen American casualties. The Californios probably suffered over one hundred casualties.

Commodore Robert F. Stockton helped Captain Frémont and Colonel Kearny take over California.

The next day, the Americans continued their march on Los Angeles. Once again the Californios attacked them, this time at La Mesa on the outskirts of Los Angeles. And once again, the American artillery dispersed them. On January 10, 1847, the Americans entered Los Angeles. By this time, the Californios realized that further resistance was useless. The struggle for California was finally over. A major portion of the land that Americans had wanted under Manifest Destiny had been acquired by the efforts of a relatively small band of hardy soldiers, sailors, and marines.[7]

Hurrah for Old Kentuck! That's the way to do it.

—Zachary Taylor shouting to the 2nd Kentucky Regiment on seeing
them rally in battle at Buena Vista, Mexico, on February 23, 1847

From Monterrey to Buena Vista

General Zachary Taylor, whose Army of Occupation was still working to advance toward Mexico City, knew that capturing Monterrey would not be easy. Attacking from the north meant taking the Black Fort, while attacking from the east meant capturing the forts of El Tenería and El Diablo. Even to get close to these three forts, Taylor's men would have to march out in the open, where they could easily be hit by enemy fire. Only on the west side of Monterrey could such dangerous marching be avoided. The Bishop's Palace sat atop a steep hill covered with chaparral. The Americans might be able to sneak up the hill, under cover of the chaparral, and capture the palace without suffering too many casualties. Then they could place their guns in the palace and fire on the city and the other forts. From the palace they could also control the road to Saltillo, the primary route by which the Mexican Army of the North received reinforcements and supplies. Taking command of that road would isolate Monterrey from the rest of Mexico, which might make the Mexicans surrender the city.[1]

The Battle of Monterrey

With this plan in mind, Taylor split his army into two groups. The smaller group, General William J. Worth's brigade of about two thousand men, was sent to slip past the Black Fort and attack the Bishop's Palace to the west of Monterrey. Meanwhile, Taylor created a diversion with his other three brigades by attacking El Tenería and El Diablo on the other side of town.

Worth's men spent most of September 20, 1846, getting into position to attack the palace. After a skirmish (minor battle) with some Mexican cavalry, Worth's men reached the base of the Mountain of Obispado, atop which sat the Bishop's Palace. At this point, Worth realized that the palace would be easier to capture if his men first took El Soldado, the fort that defended the south side of Monterrey. Federacion Hill, on which El Soldado stood, was not as well defended as the Mountain of Obispado, and El Soldado would serve as a good place to mount artillery for the assault against the palace. Also, since it was south of the palace, controlling El Soldado would permit the Americans to attack the palace from three sides.

General William J. Worth led forces through some of the most critical battles of the Mexican War.

While about half of Worth's brigade created a diversion by attacking the palace, the other half set off to attack El Soldado. It took them most of the day to work their way up through the thick chaparral on Federacion Hill's steep west slope while its defenders fired down on them. But by late afternoon, the Americans had reached the top of the hill and captured a nine-pounder from the Mexicans. When this gun was turned on the fort, El Soldado's two hundred defenders panicked and fled. On their first day of fighting, Worth's men had captured El Soldado and Federacion Hill while suffering minimal casualties.[2]

Meanwhile, the main part of the American Army was having great difficulty attacking the fortifications to

Monterrey's east. As part of his diversion in support of Worth, Taylor ordered an artillery barrage against the Black Fort. He also sent Colonel John Garland's brigade of about twelve hundred men to attack El Tenería, which was defended by two hundred Mexicans. This attack quickly bogged down when the Americans encountered deadly fire from El Tenería as well as from El Diablo, the Black Fort, and the rooftops of many houses. But rather than fall back after putting on a show as Taylor had intended him to do, Garland pressed forward with his attack. By day's end, his men had captured El Tenería, but they had to be reinforced by General John A. Quitman's brigade, and they suffered heavy casualties in the process.[3]

Taylor's last brigade, commanded by General Thomas L. Hamer, tried to force its way into the north end of town. Caught in the crossfire between the guns of the Black Fort and the musket fire from rooftops, Hamer's men also suffered heavy casualties while being repulsed several times. Altogether, Garland's, Quitman's, and Hamer's brigades suffered almost four hundred killed and wounded on the first day of battle.[4]

The first day's fighting had a sobering effect on the Americans. Although none of them had believed that capturing Monterrey would be easy, neither had they believed it would be as difficult as it turned out to be. The high casualties and lack of success shocked and demoralized the men of Garland's, Quitman's, and Hamer's brigades so much that Taylor had to keep them out of action on the second day.[5]

Fortunately for the Americans, Worth's men were still ready and able to fight. When they woke on September 22, the second day of battle, it was rainy and windy on the Mountain of Obispado. A detachment of Worth's brigade took advantage of the bad weather and the predawn darkness to creep up through the thick chaparral on the mountain's west slope. They were not seen until they reached the top, and they quickly chased away the Mexican defenders.

Some American artillerymen then dragged a twelve-pounder up the mountain and opened fire on the Bishop's Palace, while about one thousand infantrymen scrambled up the mountain and stormed the palace. Meanwhile, other artillerymen opened fire on the palace from El Soldado. In desperation, the palace's two hundred Mexican defenders charged the American infantry position, but most were either cut down or forced to flee. By late afternoon, Worth's men, who had suffered only thirty-two casualties in two days, were in complete control of the palace. They were now in an excellent position to swoop down on Monterrey from the west.

The loss of the Bishop's Palace had as bad an effect on General Pedro de Ampudia, commander of the Mexican Army defending Monterrey, as the first day of battle had had on the Americans. Although his men were still eager to fight and had demonstrated the ability to hold Monterrey, Ampudia realized that he was now cut off from reinforcements and supplies. Worse, he might have to fight his way out of Monterrey. He also feared that American artillery posted at the palace and El Soldado

Pedro de Ampudia was the Mexican general who faced the Americans at the Battle of Monterrey.

would slowly pound his troops in the city to pieces. In a fit of panic and despite his soldiers' pleas to be allowed to hold their positions, he ordered his men to abandon El Diablo and the city's outer buildings and to join him in downtown Monterrey. Ampudia then began planning for a breakout attack (when a surrounded army tries to fight its way through enemy lines).[6]

On September 23, Garland's, Quitman's, and Hamer's American brigades began probing Monterrey's north and east defenses. Although they still drew fire from the Mexicans in the Black Fort, they were greatly relieved to find that the city's rooftop defenders had pulled back and were no longer fighting as ferociously as they had two days earlier. Several detachments were able to penetrate the Mexican defenses to within a block of the city's central plaza. Satisfied that the city could now be taken, General Taylor sent some of Quitman's men to occupy El Diablo. Then he pulled the rest of the three brigades back from their probing attacks on the city, and prepared to assault the city the next day.

While the rest of the army was probing Monterrey's defenses, Worth's brigade heard the gunfire from the fighting in the city below and charged down the Mountain of Obispado into the west end of Monterrey. The infantry fought from house to house, while the artillerymen set up a large mortar (short-barreled cannon without wheels) in the Campo Santo Cemetery and began shelling the central plaza.

By now, Ampudia had had enough. Cut off from reinforcements and supplies and surrounded on three sides by enemy artillery, on September 24, he sent one of his officers under a flag of truce to ask Taylor what his terms of surrender would be. After much negotiating, the two sides agreed that the Mexican Army of the North would be allowed to leave Monterrey in peace. However, the army could take with it no weapons other than six artillery guns and the officers' swords and pistols. In addition, the two sides agreed to an eight-week truce so that their governments could work out a permanent peace settlement. By the end of September, the Mexicans had departed. Monterrey was in the hands of the United States Army.

American Strategy Reconsidered

The official American reaction to Taylor's victory at Monterrey was mixed. General Winfield Scott, the United States Army's general in chief, called the battle "three glorious days." President James K. Polk, on the other hand, responded negatively. Unimpressed with the victory, he was furious that Taylor had let Ampudia's army escape. He was also angry that Taylor had exceeded his authority by signing a truce.[7]

Taylor's situation caused Polk and Scott to rethink their basic strategy for winning the war, which was to march due south from Texas to Mexico City. Despite their victory, Taylor's men were almost completely exhausted. The farther they got from the Rio Grande, the harder it was to supply and reinforce them. There were still almost one thousand miles of mountainous terrain between them and Mexico City. And the Mexican Army of the North, although disarmed for the moment, could easily round up enough weapons to make it a powerful fighting force once again, especially if a skillful general could be found to lead it. Clearly, it was time for the Americans to come up with a new plan for the conquest of Mexico.

The Return of Santa Anna

While the Americans rested in Monterrey, the Mexicans scrambled to come up with a way to drive them out of the country. In desperation, the Mexican government turned once again to Antonio López de Santa Anna, one of the most remarkable figures in Mexican history.

Santa Anna had served in the army since the age of sixteen. He helped the Mexicans gain their independence from Spain in 1821, then helped keep the Spanish from regaining Mexico in 1829. From 1833 to 1836, he served as president of Mexico. When Texas revolted in 1836, he led the Mexican Army that won at the Alamo and Goliad but lost at San Jacinto. He was captured at San Jacinto, shipped off to Washington, D.C., as a prisoner of war, and eventually returned by the United States to Mexico.

General Antonio López de Santa Anna gained control of the Mexican government after he freed it from Spanish rule. He opposed American interference with any Mexican territory.

In 1838, the French Army captured Veracruz, the main Mexican port on the Gulf of Mexico, in an effort to get the Mexican government to pay its debts to France. Santa Anna led the troops that forced the French to leave Veracruz, and in the fighting, one of his legs was blown off. Hailed as a hero, he became president of Mexico for a second time in 1841. After just three years in office, he was driven out by his political enemies in 1844 and forced to leave the country. In 1846, he managed to get the Americans to sneak him into Mexico after the war broke out, promising he would work for a peace treaty favorable to the United States. Upon his return to Mexico, he was hailed as a hero once again. Most people believed he was the only Mexican general who could force the Americans out of Mexico. In 1846, he was made president of Mexico for a third time. Once again, he took personal control of the Mexican military—this time, to get rid of the American Army of Occupation.

Santa Anna was filled with energy, imagination, and optimism. Where others saw the end, he saw only a new beginning. He loved fancy uniforms and spectacular parades. His personal magnetism and impressive skills as a public speaker won him the affection and support of the Mexican upper class. His fondness for drinking and gambling won him the admiration and support of the Mexican lower class, including the military men who served under him. His hero was Napoleon Bonaparte, the legendary French general who almost conquered all of Europe. Santa Anna was pleased and proud to be known in Mexico as "the Napoleon of the West."[8]

On September 28, 1846, Santa Anna headed north from Mexico City with a small army. By October 8, he had reached San Luis Potosi, about three hundred miles south of Monterrey. Here, he met up with the retreating Army of the North. He immediately relieved Ampudia and made himself the army's new commander. Then he spent the next few months rebuilding the Army of the North into an effective fighting force.

The Battle of Buena Vista

While Santa Anna was transforming the Army of the North, American General Zachary Taylor was making some changes in his army as well. He wanted to explore the terrain south of Monterrey to see if he could march through it to Mexico City. He sent Worth's brigade to Saltillo, about fifty miles southwest of Monterrey, to check out the area. He also sent the brigades of Garland (now commanded by General David E. Twiggs) and Quitman marching toward the Mexican port of Tampico on the Gulf of Mexico. These troops were to help the United States Navy's Home Squadron capture Tampico for use as a naval base. The two brigades were partially replaced in Taylor's force by General John E. Wool's brigade of thirteen hundred regular soldiers and volunteers. Wool's men and Hamer's brigade, now commanded by General William O. Butler, remained with Taylor in Monterrey.

By mid-January 1847, Santa Anna had an army of more than fifteen thousand men. On January 28, he began marching it north to attack Taylor. At the same time,

Taylor's army of forty-eight hundred was slowly advancing toward Agua Nueva, about twenty miles south of Saltillo, as part of his plan to march into the heart of Mexico. The two armies would battle it out at Buena Vista.

Advance units of the two armies first made contact on February 20 at Agua Nueva, which sat in the middle of a broad valley. It was a bad place for an outnumbered army to defend. So Taylor pulled his men back to La Angostura, a narrow pass in the mountains just south of the village of Hacienda de Buena Vista, about six miles south of Saltillo.

Worth's brigade was posted to defend the two main routes through the mountains to Buena Vista. The 1st Illinois and 3rd Indiana volunteer regiments guarded the main road from San Luis Potosi to Saltillo. At the same time, the 2nd Indiana, 2nd Illinois, and 2nd Kentucky volunteer regiments guarded a pass to the east of the road. Both positions were supported with artillery. However, a third route, a pass farther to the east of the road, was foolishly left undefended. Taylor held Wool's brigade in reserve and left Butler's brigade to guard the army's rear.

Santa Anna's men were nearly exhausted by the time they reached the battlefield. He had marched them hard for days, barely giving them time enough to get a drink of water. But rather than rest his troops, he hurried to attack the hated Americans. The Americans, on the other hand, though outnumbered, were rested and ready to fight.

Santa Anna planned to attack the Americans in three places. He sent two divisions under Generals Santiago

Blanco and Francisco Mejia against the two volunteer regiments defending the road to Saltillo. Then he sent two divisions under Generals Manuel Lombardini and Francisco Pacheco to attack the three regiments in the pass. He also sent Pedro de Ampudia, former commander of the Army of the North, into the unguarded pass with two brigades of infantry and cavalry. He held the rest of his army in reserve.

The battle began on the afternoon of February 22. Blanco's men skirmished with the 1st Illinois, but with little effect. Meanwhile, Ampudia's men were progressing unseen through the unguarded pass. An American patrol finally discovered them late in the afternoon, and Taylor sent the 1st Arkansas and 1st Kentucky cavalry regiments to head them off. After several hours of fighting, Ampudia's men were driven back. Believing (incorrectly, as it turned out) that the Mexicans would not try to approach through the pass again, Taylor sent the two American cavalry units to join the three regiments defending the other pass.[9]

The battle was decided on February 23. Blanco's men resumed their attack along the road to Saltillo but they were repulsed by the 1st Illinois and several batteries of flying artillery. Lombardini's and Pacheco's men, however, managed to rout the 2nd Indiana and the two cavalry regiments and outflank the 2nd Illinois. They were breaking through the center of the American line when they were halted temporarily by a furious barrage from several batteries of flying artillery. This gave the 1st Mississippi Regiment, which had charged into the gap left by the

General Santa Anna renounced his peace agreement with the United States and then fought Zachary Taylor's troops at Hacienda de Buena Vista.

retreating Americans, time to rally the 2nd Indiana and hold the American position. Supported by the flying artillery, the Mississippi volunteers actually forced Lombardini's and Pacheco's divisions to fall back.

After a brief lull in the fighting, Santa Anna sent a reserve division commanded by General José María Ortega along the same undefended route that Ampudia had followed the day before. Once again, an American patrol discovered the move before Ortega's men could outflank the Americans. This time, Taylor sent the 1st Mississippi, the 3rd Indiana, and the flying artillery to stop them. After the American artillery routed the Mexicans, the 1st Mississippi charged after them with their Bowie knives, which were long and sharp like bayonets, and cut many of the Mexicans to pieces.

By now, the Mexican force seemed exhausted. Taylor decided to order his men to attack. But once the Mexicans saw how few Americans there were, they rallied and returned to the attack. Once again, the Americans fell back, and once again, the flying artillery saved the day. After several more hours of furious fighting, both sides had had enough. By nightfall, the battlefield was quiet.

The Mexicans had hurt Taylor's army badly. Seven hundred Americans had been killed or wounded, and another fifteen hundred were missing and presumed to have deserted. Had the Mexicans been able to attack with vigor the next day, they might have destroyed Taylor's army. But the Americans had hurt Santa Anna's army even worse. Eighteen hundred Mexicans were killed or wounded, another three hundred had been captured, and a large number (to this day, no one knows exactly how many) were missing. During the night, Taylor received supplies and reinforcements from Butler's brigade in Saltillo. Now he had as many men and as much ammunition as he had before the Battle of Buena Vista. Santa Anna's army, on the other hand, was worn out and its supplies were just about gone. When morning broke, the Americans discovered that the Mexicans had left. Instead of pursuing them, Taylor marched his army back to Monterrey. It would remain there for the rest of the war.

The field was literally covered with the dead and wounded from our artillery and the unerring fire of our riflemen. Night put a stop to the carnage, the battle having commenced around three o'clock.

—Colonel Alexander Doniphan at Chihuahua, Mexico, on March 4, 1847

6 Doniphan's Epic March

Thousands of soldiers on both sides of the Mexican War endured long marches under difficult conditions. However, none of them went on a march more remarkable than the one taken by the 1st Missouri Mounted Infantry Regiment. Led by Colonel Alexander Doniphan, this volunteer unit rode from Independence, Missouri, to Buena Vista, Mexico, a journey of over three thousand miles. Their journey took them across deserts and over mountains, and all along the way, they fought American Indians and Mexicans who usually outnumbered them.

The Missourians were interesting characters. They refused to wear uniforms because they preferred the buckskin and leather clothing of frontiersmen, which

Alexander Doniphan led American troops in one of the most daring campaigns of the Mexican War.

many of them were. They rarely bathed or cleaned up their camp. They absolutely refused to act like soldiers. They never saluted, posted sentries, or drilled. And their leader was the most unusual character of them all. Alexander Doniphan was a trial lawyer by trade. He stood over six feet six inches tall and weighed 240 pounds. His most unusual characteristic was his leadership style. Instead of always giving his men orders, he let them vote on matters of major importance. Because he respected them, they trusted and followed him without question.[1]

Doniphan and his eight hundred fifty men left Independence in June 1846 as part of Stephen Kearny's

Army of the West. After conquering New Mexico without firing a shot, Kearny decided to send Doniphan's men to General John E. Wool. Wool's brigade was marching from San Antonio, Texas, to capture Chihuahua, capital of the Mexican state of Chihuahua. Kearny thought Wool might have a greater need for the Missourians than he did in the West.[2]

Just as Doniphan's men were leaving to join Wool, a band of Apache Indians began attacking white settlers in New Mexico. Kearny sent the Missourians to subdue them before continuing on to Mexico. From early October until early December 1846, the 1st Missouri chased Apaches through the snow-covered mountains until the Apache grew tired of running and agreed to make peace. Finally, on December 16, Doniphan's men left New Mexico for Chihuahua, about five hundred miles away.

About thirty miles north of El Paso (in modern-day Texas), where the Brazito River flows into the Rio Grande, the Missourians were surprised and attacked on Christmas Day by twelve hundred Mexican cavalrymen under the command of Colonel Ponce de Leon. But as the Mexicans charged, Doniphan's infantrymen mowed them down with deadly accurate rifle fire. The Mexicans suffered one hundred casualties without ever getting close enough to kill even one American.

The 1st Missouri rested in El Paso for about six weeks, waiting for a volunteer artillery unit from Missouri to join them. Once it arrived in early February 1847, the Missourians set off for Chihuahua once again. But instead of getting easier, the journey got tougher.

One night, Navajo Indians raided their camp, killing two guards and stealing much of the regiment's food. Then the Missourians crossed over sixty miles of desert so barren that the only wildlife they saw were poisonous snakes and tarantulas. And on February 28, before they could get to Chihuahua and rest, they ran into another, larger Mexican force.

Spies had told the Mexican authorities that the Missourians were coming, and General Pedro García Condé was sent from Mexico City to defend Chihuahua. He marched his army of three hundred men and ten artillery pieces fifteen miles north of Chihuahua to the small ranching community of Rancho Sacramento. He positioned his men just north of the Sacramento River on a plateau overlooking the road along which Doniphan's men were traveling. It was an excellent defensive position from which to defend the road.

But Doniphan outfoxed García Condé. He and his men left the road long before reaching the plateau. The same scouts who had discovered García Condé's position also found a way through the hills to the west of Rancho Sacramento, which put Doniphan's regiment in the rear of García Condé's men. Once there, Doniphan's artillery opened fire and blasted the Mexicans. By the time the Battle of the Sacramento was over, the Mexicans had suffered three hundred killed and three hundred wounded, while the Americans suffered only two killed and seven wounded.[3]

The 1st Missouri entered Chihuahua without meeting further resistance on March 1. By now, they knew that Wool's brigade had been sent to join Taylor at Saltillo, so the Missourians rested until April 28 before pressing on once again, this time for Saltillo. On May 11, they reached Parras, where a band of Lipan Indians had just raided a nearby Mexican ranch. Doniphan's men disliked Indians even more than they disliked Mexicans, so they chased down the Lipan and freed the women and children the raiders had kidnapped. Then Doniphan's regiment moved on until it made contact on May 21 with some outposts of Taylor's Army of Occupation at Buena Vista.

Between June 1846 and May 1847, Doniphan's men had traveled almost thirty-five hundred miles, and they stayed on the go almost the entire time. Their terms of enlistment ended a few days after they reached Buena Vista, and they returned to Missouri where they received heroes' welcomes.[4]

Throughout the war, Americans and Mexicans alike endured miserable conditions and fought in the face of a determined enemy. Doniphan's Epic March is the most famous example of bravery and determination in the face of hardship displayed by these men.

Horrible, indeed, was the descent by that narrow and rocky path, where thousands rushed, disputing the passage with desperation, and leaving a track of blood upon the road. All classes being confounded, all military distinction and respect were lost, the badges of rank became marks for sarcasms. . . . The enemy, now masters of our camp, turned their guns upon the fugitives.

—Ramón Alacaraz of the Mexican Army remarking on the Battle of Cerro Gordo

7 From Veracruz to Puebla

 After the Battle of Monterrey, President James K. Polk and General Winfield Scott became convinced that General Zachary Taylor's Army of Occupation could not capture Mexico City by marching south from Monterrey. So they devised a new plan. While Taylor's army occupied northeastern Mexico, Scott would land a second army at Veracruz on the Gulf of Mexico and march west to Mexico City.

In terms of personality, Scott was the opposite of Taylor. Taylor liked to wear old dowdy clothes, but Scott loved to dress in fancy uniforms. Taylor had an "aw shucks" kind of speaking style, but Scott spoke in a very melodramatic way. A Boston newspaper obituary said, rather unkindly, that Scott "acts like a god and talks like

Major General Winfield Scott was General-in-Chief of the United States Army during the war with Mexico.

a fool."[1] Taylor could relate to the common soldier, but Scott could not and did not want to. Scott was so particular about every little thing being done exactly the right way that his troops called him "Old Fuss and Feathers." But in terms of military leadership, Scott was as good a general as Taylor, maybe even better.[2]

Scott's plan to end the war was a good one for several reasons. First, Veracruz is only about two hundred miles from Mexico City. This is about one third the distance between Monterrey, where Taylor was, and the Mexican capital. Second, Veracruz was connected to Mexico City by a good road called the National Highway. This road was much better than the ones on which Taylor would have to travel. Third, the United States Navy could supply and reinforce Scott's army through Veracruz. His supply lines would never be longer than two hundred miles. Taylor's supply lines, on the other hand, were already stretched much too thin. Army wagon trains on the route between the Rio Grande and Monterrey were already being attacked by Mexican cavalry, bandits, and American Indians. Since Mexico City was almost one thousand miles from Texas, this problem would only get worse as Taylor got farther into Mexico.

However, there were two major problems with Scott's plan. Veracruz was heavily fortified and the Mexicans would almost certainly oppose any landing there. And in order for the landing to work, Scott estimated that he needed twelve thousand men, fifty large transport ships to carry them, and one hundred forty small landing craft to get them from ship to shore. Scott was planning to conduct the largest amphibious landing (when ships unload troops on a beach under enemy fire) that the world had ever seen.

The Veracruz Landing

As it turned out, the landing was easier to execute than anyone predicted. Scott did not leave Washington, D.C., until late November 1846. By early March 1847, the expedition was ready to sail for Veracruz. Getting the men was no problem. Volunteer regiments had eagerly joined the army in the wake of Taylor's victories. Scott simply had eight thousand new volunteers sent to his staging area on Lobos Island off the coast of Texas in the Gulf of Mexico. The remaining four thousand men he got from Taylor's army. In mid-February, he had them transported by ship from Tampico to Lobos Island. The biggest problem was getting all the ships and landing craft together in the same place at the same time. This problem was neatly solved by the army's Quartermaster

The amphibious attack that began near the port city Veracruz was the largest troop landing in history up to that time.

General, Thomas S. Jesup. Since the United States military had no troop transport ships, Jesup simply chartered enough merchant ships to carry Scott's troops. In New Orleans, Jesup supervised the construction of surfboats (double-ended, broad-beamed, flat-bottomed landing craft) designed by Lieutenant George M. Totten to carry the troops from the ships to the beach.[3]

Scott's expedition left Lobos Island on March 2. After a week at sea, the troops began landing on March 9. Rather than assault Veracruz directly from the shore under the guns of the city's forts, Scott decided to land his men on Collada Beach, about two miles south of Veracruz. The landing itself was a bit tricky. Scott's men had to move from their transports into navy ships to be carried close to the shore, then they had to move from the navy ships into the surfboats for the trip to the beach. Except for a few rounds fired from the guns of one of the forts, the Mexicans offered no resistance. By the end of the day, all of the troops had landed without suffering a single casualty.

Rather than attack Veracruz with his infantry, Scott decided to surround the city and then bombard it with artillery. He had his men dig a trench around Veracruz from Collada Beach to Vergara, about two miles north of the city. This trench was just out of range of the guns in the city's forts. Then he had his men set up the heavy artillery behind the trench and begin shelling the city. For five days, the American guns pounded Veracruz mercilessly. Finally, on March 27, the five-thousand-man Mexican garrison surrendered. Scott and his men had

The American forces of General Winfield Scott landed at Veracruz with the naval help of Matthew Perry and his forces.

pulled off one of the most ambitious military undertakings to date and made it look easy. The road to Mexico City, and victory, now seemed to be wide open for the Americans.

While Scott's army besieged Veracruz, Mexican General Antonio López de Santa Anna's army was returning to San Luis Potosi. Although Santa Anna had lost to the Americans at Buena Vista, he had managed to scare them so badly that Taylor's Army of Occupation did not leave Monterrey for the rest of the war. This left Santa Anna free to concentrate on beating Scott.[4]

The Battle of Cerro Gordo

Before Santa Anna could stop Scott, he had to rebuild his army—again. The Army of the North lost more men to desertion during its retreat from Buena Vista than it had during the battle.

At the beginning of the Battle of Buena Vista, Santa Anna's army had fifteen thousand men, but by the time it reached San Luis Potosi, it had only about six thousand. To make up for this decrease, Santa Anna gathered conscripts, local militias, and national guardsmen. Within a very short time, his new army, the Army of the East (so called because it was headed to fight in eastern Mexico), had twelve thousand men.[5]

As Scott moved eighty-five hundred of his men up the National Highway from Veracruz, Santa Anna's army hurried down the National Highway from Mexico City. Santa Anna planned to defend the road at a mountain pass a few miles east of the village of Cerro Gordo, about fifty miles west of Veracruz. It was a good place for a defending army. Steep hills overlooked the National Highway on both sides. To the south of the road ran the Del Plan River, which made Santa Anna's right flank even more secure. To the north of the road were many gullies and much thick chaparral. Any attack from this angle would be very difficult for the Americans. To the east of the pass were three cliffs from which artillery could pound anything moving up the road. Santa Anna placed his artillery on these cliffs, the bulk of his troops in the hills, and held the rest of his men in reserve in Cerro Gordo.

Advance scouts of both armies skirmished on April 11, and the Americans came to a halt. Although the Mexican position looked unbeatable, American engineers found a narrow path through the gullies and chaparral to the north of the Mexican position that eventually came out behind the Mexican lines. Scott decided to have his engineers widen the path so he could send the main attack along this path. Meanwhile, the rest of the army would distract the artillery to the east of the pass.

For six days, American engineers widened the path. Then, on April 17, Scott sent General David E. Twiggs's division down the path while the rest of the army created a diversion by attacking the Mexican artillery positions on the cliffs. Twiggs's men got past the Mexican artillery without being seen. Before they could bypass the main body of Mexican troops, however, they were spotted and attacked. After a full day of fierce fighting, Twiggs's advance was halted.[6]

On April 18, Scott reinforced Twiggs with General William J. Worth's division and the attack began again. While most of Twiggs's and Worth's men turned off the path to attack the left flank of the Mexican position, General James Shields's three-hundred-man brigade continued down the path and got completely around the Mexican position. His men made it all the way to the National Highway at Cerro Gordo before they were attacked by Mexican troops. In Cerro Gordo, they ran into Santa Anna's reserves—about two thousand men.

These troops forced Shields's men to retreat back down the path.

But while Santa Anna's reserves were repulsing the American surprise attack, the rest of the Army of the East heard that a large part of the American Army had bypassed the Mexican Army's main position. This report threw the Mexicans into a panic. Thinking that thousands of Americans would soon be surrounding them, many Mexican soldiers began to flee. Before long the entire Army of the East was retreating as fast as it could from Cerro Gordo. Santa Anna himself left the field so quickly that some Illinois volunteers were able to capture Santa Anna's personal carriage. In it was one of his spare wooden legs. For many years, this wooden leg was displayed as a trophy of war in the Illinois State Capitol.[7]

The Battle of Cerro Gordo was a major disaster for the Mexicans. While American casualties were about four hundred killed and wounded, more than one thousand Mexicans were killed or wounded and over three thousand were taken prisoner. The army that Santa Anna had worked so hard to rebuild was shattered. What was left of it retreated all the way back to Mexico City. It would not reappear in the field until the Americans were on the outskirts of the Mexican capital. Worst of all, the Mexican Army had failed again to defeat a smaller American force. Many Mexicans began to wonder if they ever would.[8]

Problems for the Americans

But while the Mexicans faced major problems, so did the Americans. As Scott's army pushed further inland, it became clear that keeping the troops supplied would not be as easy as Polk and Scott had hoped. The Americans did not have enough wagons and mules to keep supplies moving on a regular basis from Veracruz to the front lines. Also, Mexican guerrillas (volunteer soldiers who make random attacks on an enemy) harassed the supply trains so much that the American wagon trains required heavy armed escorts. Scott's men were already outnumbered. He was afraid that taking men away from the main body to serve as escorts would make the army too weak to capture Mexico City.[9]

In addition to having problems keeping his men supplied, Scott also had a problem just keeping soldiers in his army. Three thousand of his men were volunteers whose one-year enlistments ran out just after the Battle of Cerro Gordo. By law, these men could reenlist, but they could not be forced to do so. Some of them did reenlist, but most were tired of the hardships of war. They chose to go home instead. Fortunately for Scott, he received some reinforcements from Veracruz. Even so, his entire army now numbered only about seven thousand men.

Despite these problems, Scott decided to press on toward Mexico City. After resting for two weeks in Jalapa, just four miles west of Cerro Gordo, the Americans resumed their westward march. On May 15, they entered Puebla, about seventy-five miles east of Mexico City, without a fight.

Scott rested his army at Puebla for three months. During this time, he was reinforced with a large number of volunteers. His army now contained fourteen thousand men.

While in Puebla, Scott also made an important decision. He realized he could not keep open his supply lines to Veracruz without leaving troops in each of the little towns along the way to police the road, but he also knew that doing this would weaken his army so much that it would not be able to capture Mexico City. So Scott decided to stop worrying about his supply lines. From now on, his army would live off the land. Every day, a number of American troops would be sent out into the countryside and local marketplaces to round up enough cattle, chickens, corn, beans, and water to fill the army's needs for the next day. This plan was a daring gamble, because Scott did not know for sure that he would find enough supplies to keep his army alive and strong. However, living off the land would make it possible for his army to get to Mexico City faster, where he hoped to end the war by winning a huge victory.[10]

...for this difficult operation [taking Chapultepec] we were not entirely ready, and moreover we might altogether neglect the castle, if, as we then hoped...the distant southern approaches of the city were more eligible [than] *this south southwestern approach.*

> —General Scott quoted in "Chapultepec and the Garitas of Mexico," *Southern Quarterly Review,* January, 1853

8 From Puebla to Mexico City

 While General Winfield Scott rested in Puebla, General Antonio López de Santa Anna busied himself raising a defensive army for the third time that year. He salvaged thirty-five hundred men from the remains of the Army of the East, rounded up another four thousand stragglers from the remains of the old Army of the North, and called in General Juan Alvarez's twenty-five-hundred-man Army of the South, which had been harassing Scott's supply lines. To these men Santa Anna added ten thousand militiamen and ten thousand recruits he was able to round up in and around Mexico City. By the time he was done, he had an army of thirty thousand men, more than twice the number the American Army had.

On August 7, Scott's men began marching from Puebla to Mexico City. The army was divided into four divisions, commanded by Generals David Twiggs, William Worth, John A. Quitman, and Gideon J. Pillow. The army met little resistance until it crossed the mountain range that separates eastern Mexico from the Valley of Mexico. The valley is the heartland of Mexico. It had been home to the ancient Aztec Empire, and it was home to the capital and largest city in Mexico. At its highest, the pass over the mountains is ten thousand feet above sea level. From this vantage point, the Americans could clearly see the breathtaking view of the one-hundred-twenty-mile-long valley and the three large lakes rimming Mexico City to the south.

Up to this point, Scott's army had been following the National Highway. About twenty-five miles from Mexico City, however, Scott found out that the road was heavily defended at El Penon, a mountain just outside the capital. So Scott sent his men on a branch of the National Highway that approached the city from the south rather than the east.

The Battle of Padierna/Contreras

At the village of San Agustin, about eight miles south of Mexico City, the branch road reached Mount Zacatepec. The mountain was surrounded by the Pedregal, a large lava field that had been created over thousands of years by the volcanic activity of Mount Zacatepec. The solid lava was hard, sharp, and jagged. It was very difficult and dangerous to cross.

Scott tried first to go around the Pedregal by following the branch road, which circled the lava field to the east. But on August 18, Worth's division, which was leading the march, ran into heavy Mexican resistance at the village of San Antonio. Scott ordered Worth to halt his advance. Then he sent Twiggs's and Pillow's divisions, about five thousand men, to the west of the Pedregal along a narrow trail through Padierna and San Geronimo (the Americans mistakenly thought San Geronimo was Contreras, a village two miles west of Padierna). These two divisions were to continue all the way around the Pedregal and come out behind the Mexicans in San Antonio so that Worth's men could continue their advance.

When Twiggs's and Pillow's divisions reached Padierna on August 19, they ran into five thousand men commanded by Mexican General Gabriel Valencia. The two sides engaged in an all-day artillery battle. Late in the day, some Americans were able to slip around the Mexican left flank and reached San Geronimo. Some of them even managed to get behind the Mexican position. Then, as night fell, they discovered that they were trapped between Valencia's men in Padierna and Santa Anna's main army in San Angel, just two miles away.[1]

Had Santa Anna attacked in the morning with the main body of his army, he probably would have destroyed the two American divisions. Almost certainly, this would have destroyed Scott's army and ended the war in Mexico's favor. General Valencia was so sure this would happen that he threw a great feast that night, during

Personal differences may have led to Santa Anna's abandonment of General Valencia (seen here) and his troops.

which he promoted all his officers. Instead, Santa Anna retreated to the north toward Mexico City, leaving Valencia's men to fight the Americans alone. No one knows for sure why Santa Anna did this. The most likely reason is that he hated Valencia, who was one of his most bitter political rivals. In 1844, Valencia had helped remove Santa Anna from the Mexican presidency and exiled him from the country. Perhaps Santa Anna abandoned Valencia to the Americans as a way of getting revenge. Whatever the reason, the Americans benefited greatly from this piece of luck. Instead of being routed by the combined forces of Santa Anna and Valencia on the morning of August 20, the Americans attacked and defeated Valencia's men in Padierna. The Battle of Contreras, as the Americans called it, lasted twenty minutes. Seven hundred Mexicans were killed and another eight hundred taken prisoner. The Americans suffered only sixty killed and wounded.[2]

The Battle of Churubusco

As Valencia's men retreated up the road toward the capital, Twiggs's and Pillow's men pursued them. Meanwhile, Worth's division managed to outflank the Mexicans in San Antonio, which made them retreat toward Mexico City, too. With most of his army now in retreat, Santa Anna tried to keep open an escape route to the capital. A major obstacle to their retreat was the Churubusco River, which was too wide to wade across. Santa Anna posted strong defenses at the bridge at the town of Churubusco, which connected San Antonio with Mexico City. He hoped this would allow all of his men to make it into the capital, where they would be well protected behind stone walls.[3]

Scott was so intent on catching the retreating Mexicans before they reached Mexico City that he paid no attention to how well defended the river crossing was. He also failed to realize that two other bridges to the west of the Churubusco bridge were only lightly defended. Had he sent a large force across either of these bridges, he might have been able to surround the Mexicans at the Churubusco bridge, or at least force them to retreat with a minimum of casualties. Instead, he simply ordered Worth's and Pillow's men to attack the Churubusco bridge's defenders while Twiggs's men attacked the defenders holed up in the Convent of San Mateo, about five hundred yards west of the bridge.

At the bridge, the odds clearly seemed to be against the Americans, who had twenty-six hundred attackers against about eight thousand Mexican defenders. However, the Mexicans were by now tired, hungry, and demoralized from their earlier defeat that day. In fact, the entire war now seemed like a nightmare to most of the Mexican troops. It seemed that no matter how bravely they fought, they would always manage to find a way to lose. Even though they still outnumbered the Americans

American General Scott led his men against Mexican General Santa Anna along the Churubusco River in order to get to Mexico City.

and would continue to fight bravely, very few Mexican soldiers actually still expected to beat the hated Yankees.

For about two hours, bullets flew hot and heavy, with neither side giving an inch. Finally, the superior discipline and confidence of the Americans turned the tide of battle. Despite being outnumbered, the Americans fixed bayonets and charged. The Mexicans finally broke and ran away. Thirty minutes later, the convent's defenders surrendered, bringing the battle to a close.

The Battles of Padierna/Contreras and Churubusco, both of which were fought on August 20, were costly for both sides. The Americans lost more than one hundred killed and almost one thousand wounded—men they could not easily replace. The Mexicans, on the other hand, lost four thousand killed and wounded while another three thousand were captured. Although Scott's army suffered heavy losses, Santa Anna's army had been destroyed.[4]

A Temporary Truce

Santa Anna immediately sent word to Scott, asking for a truce while a peace treaty could be worked out. On August 22, Scott agreed. He knew that any peace treaty signed at this point would probably give the Americans just about everything they wanted without having to lose any more men in battle. But before the peace talks could even begin, Santa Anna violated the truce by building up the fortifications around Mexico City. On September 7, Scott began planning for the final attack of the war, this time on the Mexican capital.

Mexico City sat in the middle of a marshy plain that was too wet for an army to march over. Therefore, Scott planned to take the capital by marching from the south and west along several causeways. These long, built-up mounds of earth carried roads across the marshy plain into Mexico City. The approaches to the western causeways were defended by three imposing structures. Molino del Rey was a group of stone buildings about two hundred yards in length. Casa Mata was a large stone building five hundred yards west of Molino del Rey. And the Castle of Chapultepec was a fortified castle on top of a hill about one thousand yards east of Molino del Rey. The Americans could have bypassed these three forts, but Scott did not want to leave any Mexican strongpoints behind him. He decided to capture all three before proceeding further.[5]

The Battle for Mexico City

On the morning of September 8, 1847, Scott sent Worth's division to attack Molino del Rey. The Mexican defenders fought bravely but they were quickly outnumbered and surrounded. After about an hour of fierce fighting, they were forced to surrender.

Then, Worth's men turned their attention to Casa Mata. An artillery barrage, followed by a bayonet charge, succeeded in making its Mexican defenders flee, but only at great cost to the Americans. Between the two engagements, Worth's men suffered more than one hundred killed and almost seven hundred wounded.

The battle for Chapultepec was a crucial one. Casualties were rapidly diminishing Scott's army, and the Americans could not afford any more costly victories like the ones at Molino del Rey and Casa Mata. Not only did the Americans have to win, but they had to win without suffering very many losses. However, the castle's steep walls were two hundred feet high. The only way in would be to storm the main gate or scale the walls on ladders. Both of these options were dangerous missions for any soldier. Many Americans felt sure they could not capture Chapultepec no matter how many of them died in the attempt.[6]

The battle for Chapultepec began on the morning of September 12 with a massive artillery barrage. Scott hoped that this would make Chapultepec's defenders surrender. Although a number of Mexicans were killed during the barrage, the rest of the castle's two hundred fifty defenders refused to surrender.

The next morning, the storming and scaling parties were sent into action. Fortunately for the Americans, they were able to send up fifty scaling parties at the same time. By this time, there were not enough Mexicans left to defend against all fifty scaling parties. It was only a matter of time before the American attackers began pouring over the walls. Despite fierce fighting, Chapultepec fell to the Americans after only two hours. When the number of killed and wounded was counted at the end of the day, the Americans had suffered four hundred fifty casualties.[7]

Chapultepec's fall opened the doors of Mexico City to the Americans. Before long, two of Scott's divisions were racing down the causeways into Mexico City. By the end of the day, both divisions occupied positions inside the capital. While the exhausted Americans rested during the night, Santa Anna retreated from Mexico City with what was left of his army. On September 14, General Winfield Scott rode into the capital's Grand Plaza at the head of his crippled but victorious army.

The United States of America and the United Mexican States animated by a sincere desire to put an end to the calamities of the war which unhappily exists…have, under protection of Almighty God, the author of peace, arranged, agreed upon, and signed the following: Treaty of Peace, Friendship, Limits, and Settlement…

—Treaty of Guadalupe Hidalgo, February 2, 1848

9 Making Peace

With the capture of Mexico City, General Winfield Scott's work was almost done. Nicholas P. Trist's work, on the other hand, was just beginning. On April 10, 1847, about two weeks after Scott's army captured Veracruz, Polk sent Trist to Mexico. Trist was the chief clerk of the State Department, and he seemed to be the perfect man to work out a peace treaty with the Mexicans. He had been a cadet at the United States Military Academy at West Point. He had been a law student of former President Thomas Jefferson and a private secretary to former President Andrew Jackson. More importantly, he was an intelligent and charming person, he spoke Spanish fluently, and he had served as consul (a type of junior ambassador) in Havana, Cuba.

Nicholas Trist served as ambassador to Mexico. He was sent to negotiate a treaty with the defeated Mexican government that would win territory for the United States.

He also knew something about the ways of Latin Americans.

Trist arrived in Veracruz on May 6, 1847. He came down with a mysterious illness almost immediately and had to stay in Veracruz for several days. He caught up with General Scott in Jalapa, a town on the National Highway between Cerro Gordo and Puebla, on May 14. After some initial friction, the two men became good friends. Scott even declared (although he did not have the power to do so) that Trist was the new American minister to Mexico.

While Scott and Trist were in Jalapa, General Antonio López de Santa Anna, president of Mexico and commanding officer of the Mexican Army opposing Scott's, made the Americans a startling offer. In return for a bribe of $1 million, Santa Anna said he would be willing to end the war peacefully. Scott and Trist decided to accept the offer and paid Santa Anna $10,000. The balance would be due on the signing of a peace treaty. Unfortunately for the two Americans, they had been played for fools. Santa Anna changed his mind about talking peace, but he kept the $10,000 anyway.[1]

While in Jalapa, Trist sent a note to Jose Ramon Pacheco, the Mexican foreign minister in Mexico City, asking for a meeting. Pacheco ignored the note and refused to meet with Trist. Meanwhile, President Polk began to fear that Trist's presence in Mexico was being taken by the Mexicans as a sign of American weakness. On October 4, Polk sent Trist a letter recalling him to Washington.

By the time Trist got the letter on November 16, however, he had already opened peace talks with the new Mexican foreign minister, Manuel Peña y Peña.[2] Peña was unhappy about Trist's recall. Peña wanted peace but he felt that Mexican honor prevented him from approaching the United States to ask for it. If Trist went home as ordered, this is exactly what Peña would have to do. So he convinced Trist that, if he stayed, a peace treaty could be worked out quickly.[3]

Although the treaty did not come about quite as fast as Peña had promised, both sides began talking seriously about peace for the first time. In terms of territory, the Mexicans agreed to sell California and New Mexico to the United States. They also agreed that the new boundary between Mexico and the United States would be the Rio Grande from the Gulf of Mexico to the 32nd parallel, about thirty miles north of the present-day border between New Mexico and the Mexican state of Chihuahua. The boundary would then run due west until it hit the Gila River, then follow the river all the way to the Colorado River. Then it would follow the present-day border between California and the Mexican state of Baja California Norte.

The biggest problem the peace negotiators faced involved money. The Mexicans demanded $30 million for California and New Mexico, an amount Trist could not agree to. Finally, both sides agreed on a payment of $15 million, with the provision that the United States would also assume Mexico's debts to residents in California and New Mexico.

On February 2, 1848, in the town of Guadalupe Hidalgo just outside Mexico City, Trist and the Mexican peace commissioners ended the Mexican War by signing the Treaty of Guadalupe Hidalgo. Now the treaty would have to be ratified by the Senates of both nations in order to become official.

Many American senators were unhappy with the Treaty of Guadalupe Hidalgo. Those senators who wanted to annex all of Mexico thought the treaty was too generous to the Mexicans. Those senators who were opposed to annexing any part of Mexico thought the treaty was too unfair to the Mexicans. A number of senators opposed the treaty because Trist had written and signed it after his authority to do so had been revoked.[4]

Polk was furious that Trist had disobeyed his orders by not returning to the United States when he was recalled. But in the end, he realized that the treaty gave the United States about as much as it could expect to get without more fighting. He was able to persuade a majority of the senators to see this, too. On March 10, 1848, the United States Senate ratified the treaty.

The debate in the Mexican Senate was not quite as lengthy. No Mexican senator was happy about giving up California and New Mexico, but all of them realized that, if the war continued, Mexico might lose even more territory. So on March 25, the Mexican Senate also ratified the treaty. The Mexican War had finally come to an end. And with that end, the United States had gained all the territory it had hoped to win with its aggressive policy of Manifest Destiny.

What is this territory, Mr. President, which you propose to wrest from Mexico? It is consecrated to the heart of the Mexican by many a well-fought battle with his old Castilian master. His Bunker Hills, and Saratogas, and Yorktowns, are there! The Mexican can say, "There I bled for liberty! and shall I surrender that confiscated home of my affections to the Anglo-Saxon invaders? . . .

—U.S. Senator Thomas Corwin addressing Congress

10 How the War Affected Mexico

 The Mexican War was a disaster for Mexico. It forced the nation to surrender about 40 percent of its territory. It also badly weakened the faith of Mexicans in their government, which touched off a major struggle for reform that would go on for over twenty years. The loss of the war also increased the deep mistrust Mexicans had often felt for Americans, and made it strong enough to last for almost one hundred years.

The Loss of Territory

The Treaty of Guadalupe Hidalgo forced Mexico to give up California and New Mexico to the United States. These vast territories included modern-day California, Nevada, Utah, Arizona, and New Mexico, as well as parts

The area Mexico gave up as a result of the Mexican War covers what is now California, Nevada, Utah and parts of four other states.

of Colorado and Wyoming. At the time, these areas were not well developed economically. Fewer than one hundred thousand people lived in this huge territory, and most of them made their living by ranching, hunting, trapping, or farming. The few products this region had to trade were bought mostly by Americans, even in the years before the Mexican War. To lose these territories was not a serious blow to the Mexican economy.

However, the loss of California and New Mexico was a serious blow to Mexican pride. The Mexicans had thought of themselves as good fighters ever since 1821, when they had won their war for independence against Spain. Their pride had been hurt a little in 1836 when they lost the Texas War for Independence, but not much, since they had never fully admitted that defeat. Texas was not very big, it had been settled later than the rest of Mexico, and Mexican culture had never really taken root there. Besides, Mexican pride had been restored just two years after losing Texas, when Santa Anna's men threw out the French Army that had captured Veracruz. Losing California and New Mexico, on the other hand, hurt Mexico's national pride a lot. These places had been part of Mexico for two hundred fifty years, and Hispanic culture thrived there. These places had made up one third of Mexico's territory. It was a much greater loss than losing Texas, which was only a small percentage of Mexican territory at the time. Imagine how Americans would feel if Canada invaded the United States and captured the states of Minnesota, North and South Dakota, Montana, Idaho, Washington, and Oregon. This is how the Mexicans felt about losing California and New Mexico. Many Mexicans still feel the same way today.[1]

Of course, no Mexicans felt worse about losing these territories than those who lived in them. The Treaty of Guadalupe Hidalgo made these people American citizens, but they would not always be treated equally. After the war, the first American territorial governments prevented lifelong Mexican residents from serving in the government. Instead, these governments were controlled by newly arrived Americans, who used their influence to obtain—sometimes dishonestly—much of the land that wealthy Mexican ranchers in California and New Mexico had owned.

Mexican Americans did not go down without a fight. In 1847, an uprising in Taos, New Mexico, resulted in the deaths of the American governor and several of his officials. And in what is today Nevada, Mexican Americans successfully used force to keep American cattlemen from taking their land. By 1880, however, Mexicans living in California and New Mexico had been overpowered by a flood of newly arrived Americans. They rapidly lost their political power and economic influence.[2]

Armed Revolt

During the Mexican War, the Mexican government had to call in its soldiers and militiamen from all across Mexico to try to repel the American invaders. This meant that practically no one was left in the Mexican states to keep the American Indians who lived throughout Mexico under control, and many of the tribes revolted. After the war was over, the Indians realized that the Americans had almost totally destroyed the Mexican Army. This led to more Indian revolts.[3]

The worst Indian revolt was the Caste War (1847–1904) in Yucatan. When the Mexican War broke out, local authorities in the port city of Campeche raised a battalion of Mayan Indians to help defend against a possible American attack. The attack never came, but in 1847, the battalion revolted against the harsh treatment of Mayan Indians by the Mexican government. The revolt quickly spread across the Yucatan Peninsula, the ancestral homeland of the Mayan people. For six years, the Mayans and Mexicans battled fiercely. At one point the Mayans controlled almost the entire Yucatan Peninsula, and the major cities of Campeche and Merida were filled with non-Indian refugees. The Mayans were temporarily defeated in 1853. The conflict flared up again in 1858. This time, it took the Mexican government almost fifty years to subdue the Mayans. Even today, there is much ill feeling between Mexicans and Indians in Yucatan.[4]

American Indian revolts broke out as a result of the Mexican War in other places, too. Between 1848 and 1855, Indians revolted in the states of Oaxaca and Guerrero in the south, Veracruz in the east, Coahuila and Tamaulipas in the northeast, Chihuahua and Durango in the north, and Hidalgo and Tlaxcala in central Mexico. Indian raids were so horrible in the north that large areas were abandoned by non-Indians. Not until the late 1850s was the Mexican military strong enough to restore the government's rule in these places.

Nationalism

Even though the war gave the Mexicans very little to cheer about, it did give them some new national heroes to celebrate. The most famous ones are Los Niños Héroes, who died at the Battle of Chapultepec.

Los Niños Héroes are remembered in Mexico to this day. In 1947, a large stone monument commemorating their sacrifice was erected in the park at the base of Chapultepec Hill. Every year on September 13, the day they died fighting for their country, an impressive ceremony is held in their honor.[5]

Reform

Many educated Mexicans believed that Mexico lost the war because the country was run poorly. Although Mexico was supposed to be a democracy, most of the real power belonged to the military and the Roman Catholic Church. Every Mexican president from 1821 to 1848 had been a general, so the army got most of the money from tax revenues. In addition to owning thousands of churches and cathedrals, the Church owned a lot of houses and farms. But since the Church was tax-exempt, the government could not make tax money off any of this property. Mexico also had three different legal systems— one for soldiers, one for priests, and one for everyone else. A soldier or a priest accused of committing a civil crime would be tried in a military or a church court, not in a civil court. This meant that Mexicans were not equal before the law, which is a basic feature of democracy.

For seven years after the Mexican War ended, many educated Mexicans struggled to reform the government. Many of them were sent to jail by the government, which was still controlled by the military. Others had to flee the country. But in 1855, a group of civilian reformers took control of the government and began making changes. They changed the three-court system so that everyone received equal justice. They also tried to make the army and the Church sell any property that was not used for military or religious purposes. In 1857, they approved a new constitution that gave Mexicans most of the basic rights spelled out in the United States Constitution.[6]

The army and the Church, which lost their special privileges, were not happy about these reforms. In 1858, civil war broke out when the army tried to retake control of the government. In response, the reformers raised an army of their own from peasants and middle-class citizens who were tired of the old way of doing things. Known as the War of the Reform, this civil war raged for three years before the reformers won. They were able to win largely because many officers and soldiers left the regular army and joined the reformers' army. However, the civil war exhausted Mexico so much that it could not pay its debts to foreign countries.

In 1861, France once again landed an army in Veracruz with the intention of making Mexico a French colony until Mexican debts to France were repaid. For the next six years, the reformers fought the French until they left the country in 1867. The effort to reform Mexico had taken almost twenty years. No one knows how much it cost in terms of lives and money.[7]

Yankeephobia

The Mexican War made Mexicans hate Americans. Almost immediately after the war, a number of folk songs were written that expressed fear and hatred of Yankees, as Mexicans called all Americans. In later years, when the Mexicans undertook a major railroad construction program, none of them wanted to build a connecting line to the United States because that would give the hated Yankees easier access to Mexico. Ever since the Mexican

War, many Mexicans have blamed all their country's problems on the United States.[8]

Until 1950, the actions of the United States government did nothing to change this negative attitude. On several occasions, the United States tried to interfere in Mexico's internal affairs. The worst attempt took place between 1910 and 1917, when the United States tried to influence who would be president of Mexico.

In 1911, Francisco Madero, who belonged to one of Mexico's most powerful families, was elected president of Mexico. He seemed hostile to American business interests in Mexico, so the United States secretly gave money and weapons to the rebel forces of Victoriano Huerta, the former Commander in Chief of the Mexican Army. In 1913 Huerta's forces captured and killed Madero, and Huerta became the new president. When he also threatened American business interests, the United States shifted its support to the governor of the state of Coahuila, Venustiano Carranza. In 1914, the Americans seized Veracruz from Huerta's forces, and a few months later Carranza replaced Huerta as president. But when Carranza refused to accept American advice about who should serve in the new Mexican cabinet, the Americans began supporting Pancho Villa, a rebel military leader who had supported Madero but opposed Huerta and Carranza, for president. Unfortunately for Villa, he had little support in Mexico, so the Americans were eventually forced to accept Carranza.

This made Villa angry. In 1916, his small army began killing Americans on both sides of the United

States-Mexico border. His men pulled sixteen Americans off a train in northern Mexico and shot them. Then they raided Columbus, New Mexico, and shot seventeen more Americans.

In response, the United States government sent General John J. Pershing, who would later become a hero in World War I, into Mexico with an army to capture Villa and his men. Pershing chased Villa for three hundred miles into Mexico but never found him. However, Pershing did find a Mexican army that had been sent to stop him. The two armies fought two skirmishes during which forty Mexicans and twelve Americans died. Fortunately, Pershing's army was recalled before another war broke out.[9]

Relations between Mexico and the United States began to improve in 1947 when United States President Harry Truman visited Mexico City. While there, he laid a wreath on the monument to Los Niños Héroes. This symbolic act helped break the ice between the two countries. Not long after Truman's visit, the Congresses of Mexico and the United States voted to return all the flags and other trophies of war—including Santa Anna's wooden leg—that had been captured during the Mexican War. Then Mexican President Miguel Aleman visited Washington, and friendly relations between the countries began to develop. Problems such as immigration and trade continue to exist between the two countries, but today, Mexico and the United States seem to be on the road to becoming good neighbors, if not good friends.[10]

. . . The Southern Rebellion [American Civil War] *was largely an outgrowth of the Mexican War. Nations, like individuals, are punished for their transgressions. We got our punishment in the most . . . expensive war of modern times.*

—Ulysses S. Grant in his autobiography *Personal Memoirs*

11 How the War Affected the United States

 The Mexican War also dramatically affected the United States. By winning the war, the United States acquired a huge amount of territory, known as the Mexican Cession.

The Treaty of Guadalupe Hidalgo made the Rio Grande the boundary between the United States and Mexico. It also gave the United States the Mexican territories of California and New Mexico. These territories eventually entered the Union as the states of Arizona, California, Nevada, New Mexico, and Utah.

It would be hard to imagine the United States today without these states. California has more people than any other state in the Union. The important cities of Los Angeles, San Francisco, San Diego, Salt Lake City,

Phoenix, Las Vegas, and Santa Fe are all built on land obtained from Mexico in the war. Over the years, this area has supplied the United States with a significant amount of its gold, silver, oil, cattle, fruits, vegetables, and even movies. A number of popular tourist attractions, such as Yosemite and Sequoia National Parks, the Grand Canyon, the Las Vegas casinos, Hollywood, and Disneyland are located in these states.

Presidential Politics and the Mexican War

The war produced a number of American heroes. Some of them used the popularity they received from the Mexican War to run for president. Generals Zachary Taylor and Winfield Scott emerged from the Mexican War as national heroes. By leading their armies to victory, both men became very popular all across the United States. This popularity allowed them both to run for president. In 1848, Taylor was elected president on the Whig party ticket, but he died in office after serving only two years. In 1852, the Whigs nominated Winfield Scott for president. He lost to Franklin Pierce, the candidate of the Democrats, who had also served as a general in the Mexican War.

Although he did not win the kind of amazing, against-all-odds victories that Taylor and Scott won, John C. Frémont became famous for his exploits in California during the Mexican War. In 1856, the Republican party made him its first candidate for president. He lost the election, but the Republicans went on to become one of the two major parties in the United States.

Mexican War: A Cause of the Civil War

The biggest political issue in the United States during the 1840s and 1850s was slavery. Many Northerners wanted either to abolish slavery or to keep it confined to the Southern states, in order to protect free labor and their political power in Congress. Many were also morally opposed to the practice of slavery. Most Southerners, on the other hand, wanted to expand slavery in order to preserve the way of life they had lived for generations. The issue became an even bigger problem after the Mexican War. Neither side could agree whether slavery should be allowed into the new western territories won from Mexico during the war.

The problem of slavery in new territories had been solved through compromise. The 1820 Missouri Compromise drew an imaginary line across the Louisiana

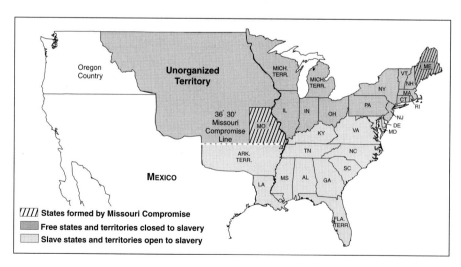

With the Missouri Compromise, the United States temporarily settled the issue of where slavery would be permitted.

Purchase territories at 36°30′ north latitude. Slavery would be permitted south of the line and prohibited north of the line, with the exception of Missouri, because Missouri's southern boundary was the compromise line and slavery had already been established there. Northerners and Southerners were happy with the Missouri Compromise—for a while.

When the United States acquired so much new territory from Mexico, the first question to arise in the nation, which was already being torn by disagreement over slavery, was whether slavery would be permitted there. In fact, the question came up in 1846 even before the war was over. David Wilmot, an antislavery congressman from Pennsylvania, asked Congress to pass a bill prohibiting slavery in any territory the United States might gain during the Mexican War. The Wilmot Proviso, as his request was called, was voted down by the Senate, but it began the long debate on the future of slavery in the Mexican Cession.

In addition to the Wilmot Proviso, three other responses to the problem were suggested. Southerners insisted that Congress did not have the power to prohibit people from taking their property or their slaves with them wherever they wanted to go. Therefore, Congress could not keep slaves, who were considered property, out of the Mexican Cession. Other people suggested extending the Missouri Compromise Line, or 36°30′, all the way to the Pacific Ocean, permitting slavery south of the line and prohibiting it north of the line. Still others argued that the residents of the Mexican Cession should be allowed to decide for themselves through a vote whether or not to permit slavery. This idea became known as popular sovereignty.

Neither of the two major political parties of the late 1840s, the Democrats and the Whigs, took a stand on the issue of slavery in the Mexican Cession. This angered antislavery members of both parties, who left to form the Free-Soil party. The Free-Soilers' major issue was keeping slavery out of the Mexican Cession. In the election of 1848, they sent ten members to Congress, and their candidate for president polled 10 percent of the popular vote.

The Compromise of 1850 solved the problem for a while by approving popular sovereignty in the new territories of Utah and New Mexico. As part of the same compromise agreement, California was admitted to the Union as a free state.

The real trouble started when the idea of popular sovereignty was applied to territories outside of the Mexican Cession. According to the Missouri Compromise, any states formed from the Kansas and Nebraska territories, which were originally part of the Louisiana Purchase, were supposed to be free from slavery. But Southerners began arguing that, if popular sovereignty could be allowed in Utah and New Mexico, then it should be allowed in Kansas and Nebraska. In 1854, Congress passed the Kansas-Nebraska Act, which set aside the Missouri Compromise so that the voters in Kansas and Nebraska could decide for themselves if theirs would be free or slave states.

Nebraska was so far north that it would probably never be a slave state. But Kansas was no farther north than Missouri, Kentucky, Virginia, and Maryland—all of which were slave states. So there was a real possibility that Kansas might vote to allow slavery. Thousands of proslavery and antislavery settlers rushed to Kansas to influence the vote. Before long, they began shooting at each other.

Many antislavery people were so outraged by the Kansas-Nebraska Act that they formed the Republican party, which opposed the spread of slavery to the territories. This party was bigger and stronger than the Free-Soil party, since it united people who wanted to prevent the spread of slavery with the abolitionists who

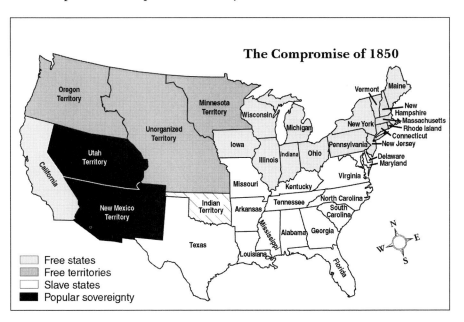

The Compromise of 1850 helped settle the problem of whether slavery would be permitted in the new western territories won from Mexico.

wanted to eliminate slavery altogether. In 1860, it succeeded in electing its candidate for the presidency,
Abraham Lincoln. When this happened, the South feared
that slavery would soon be barred from the territories and
eventually from the South as well. In order to protect the
future of slavery, eleven Southern states left the Union
and the Civil War began.

Mexican War: A Training Ground for the Civil War

At the start of the Civil War, the Confederate States of
America, made up of the Southern states that had left the
Union, chose Jefferson Davis, a former colonel of the 1st
Mississippi Regiment that helped saved the day at the
Mexican War's Battle of Buena Vista, to be its first and
only president. Like Davis, a number of Civil War
generals also got their first battlefield experience during
the Mexican War. Many of them played important roles
during the Mexican War as junior officers.

Robert E. Lee, who eventually became the commanding general of the Confederate Army, was a captain
of engineers in Mexico. He provided Zachary Taylor's and
Winfield Scott's armies with detailed reports on Mexican
defensive positions and scouted out ways to attack them.
Ulysses S. Grant, the last commanding general of the
Union Army of the Potomac, was an infantry lieutenant
in Mexico. He was cited for bravery during the fighting
at Molino del Rey. Pierre G. T. Beauregard, commander
of the Confederate forces that fired on Fort Sumter to
start the Civil War, was a lieutenant of engineers in

Abraham Lincoln was elected the sixteenth United States president in 1860. His election, however, set off tensions in the South that would ultimately lead to the Civil War.

Mexico. He served primarily as Lee's assistant while the two were assigned to Scott's army. George B. McClellan, first commanding general of the Union Army of the Potomac, was a lieutenant of engineers in Mexico. He was cited for bravery at the battles of Contreras, Churubusco, and Chapultepec.

Braxton Bragg, general of the Confederate Army of Tennessee, and George H. Thomas, general of the Union Army of Tennessee, had been lieutenants of artillery in Mexico. They commanded two of the artillery batteries that stopped the Mexican advance at the Battle of Buena Vista and helped save the day for the Americans.[1] George

G. Meade, commanding general of the Union Army of the Potomac at Gettysburg, was a lieutenant of engineers in Mexico. He was cited for bravery during the Battle of Monterrey. Thomas J. "Stonewall" Jackson, Lee's top Confederate general during the Civil War until his death in May 1863, was a lieutenant of artillery in Mexico. He was cited for bravery in just about every battle that Scott's army fought.

Captain Robert E. Lee aided the assault against the Mexicans at Veracruz. His brilliant efforts during the Mexican War would later help Lee become the commanding general of Confederate forces during the Civil War.

What Happened to Manifest Destiny?

The Mexican War put an end to Manifest Destiny for a while. For the most part, the Mexican Cession was Manifest Destiny's fulfillment. Although Americans still wanted their country to expand and grow, the sectional crisis that the Mexican War helped create took up the nation's attention for many years. In the 1890s, however, Manifest Destiny reappeared. This time, it was partly responsible for getting the United States involved in the Spanish-American War of 1898, during which the United States acquired Puerto Rico and the Philippines from Spain. But after fighting a long and bloody war with the Filipinos who wanted to be independent, Americans backed away from acquiring any more foreign territory.

Americans had mixed feelings about the Mexican War after it was over. Many thought the war was unjustifiable, and said that the United States had deliberately picked a fight with its weaker neighbor. However, the war also helped the United States expand to the size it is today and paved the way for the United States to become a dominant world power.

Timeline

1803—Louisiana Purchase made.

1819—Adams-Onis Treaty establishes boundary.

1821—Mexico wins its independence from Spain.

1836—Spain recognizes Mexico's independence; Texas declares its independence from Mexico; Battles of the Alamo, Goliad, and San Jacinto take place; Texas applies for admission to the United States.

1842—U.S. Navy occupies Monterey, California; Santa Anna returns from exile, becoming dictator of Mexico.

1844—James Polk elected president of the United States.

1845—United States tries to buy California and New Mexico from Mexico; Texas admitted to the United States.

1846—*March*: U.S. Army occupies Texas south of the Nueces River.
April: Fighting breaks out between United States and Mexico.
May 8–9: Battles of Palo Alto and Resaca de la Palma take place.
May 13: United States declares war on Mexico.
June: Bear Flag Republic declared in California.
August: American forces occupy Santa Fe, New Mexico.
September 20–24: Battle of Monterrey.
December 6: Battle of San Pasqual.
December 25: Battle of Brazito River; El Paso occupied by American forces.

1847—*January 8*: Battle of San Gabriel.

January 13: United States takes control of California.

February 22–23: Battle of Buena Vista.

February 28: Battle of Río Sacramento.

March 29: Americans capture Veracruz.

April 17–18: Battle of Cerro Gordo.

May 15–29: Americans enter Puebla.

August 19–20: Battles of Padierna/Contreras and Churubusco take place.

September 12–13: Battle of Chapultepec.

September 14: U.S. Army enters Mexico City.

1848—*February 2*: Treaty of Guadalupe Hidalgo signed.

March 10: U.S. Congress ratifies Treaty of Guadalupe Hidalgo.

May 25: Mexican Congress ratifies Treaty of Guadalupe Hidalgo.

Chapter Notes

Chapter 1. The Battle of Chapultepec

1. Alan Peskin, ed., *Volunteers: The Mexican War Journals of Private Richard Coulter and Sergeant Thomas Barclay, Company E, Second Pennsylvania Infantry* (Kent, Ohio: Kent State University Press, 1991), pp. 323–327.

2. Mark Crawford, ed., *Encyclopedia of the Mexican-American War* (Santa Barbara, Calif.: ABC-CLIO, 1999), p. 201.

3. Edward H. Moseley and Paul C. Clark, Jr., *Historical Dictionary of the United States-Mexican War* (Lanham, Md.: Scarecrow Press, 1997), pp. 244–245.

4. Peskin, pp. 165–170.

5. Crawford, p. 201.

6. Peskin, p. 170.

Chapter 2. Origins of the Mexican War

1. Texas Humanities Resource Center and the University of Texas at Arlington Library, *Invasion Yanqui: The Mexican War, 1846–1848,* <http://www.humanities-interactive.org/Invasionyanqui> (November 25, 2001).

2. Alan Brinkley, *American History: A Survey*, 10th ed. (Boston: McGraw-Hill College, 1999), p. 234.

3. John M. Murrin et al., *Liberty, Equality, Power: A History of the American People* (Fort Worth, Tex.: Harcourt Brace College Publishers, 1999), pp. 296–298.

4. Brinkley, pp. 254, 258, 430, 433, 438.

5. Murrin, pp. 435–438.

6. Brinkley, pp. 430, 437.

7. Murrin, p. 444.

8. Brinkley, p. 430.

9. Murrin, p. 442.

10. John S. D. Eisenhower, *So Far From God: The U.S. War with Mexico, 1846–1848* (New York: Random House, 1989), pp. 13–14.

11. Murrin, p. 444.

12. Brinkley, p. 438.

13. Richard Hofstadter, ed., *Great Issues in American History: From the Revolution to the Civil War, 1765–1865* (New York: Vintage Books, 1958), p. 342.

14. Murrin, pp. 444–445.

Chapter 3. From Fort Texas to Monterrey

1. K. Jack Bauer, *Zachary Taylor: Soldier, Planter, Statesman of the Old Southwest* (Baton Rouge: Louisiana State University Press, 1985), p. 94.

2. John S. D. Eisenhower, *So Far From God: The U.S. War with Mexico, 1846–1848* (New York: Random House, 1989), pp. 54–65.

3. Ibid., pp. 71–73.

4. Cecil Robinson, ed., *The View From Chapultepec: Mexican Writers on the Mexican-American War* (Tucson: University of Arizona Press, 1989), p. 46.

5. Richard B. Winders, *Mr. Polk's Army: The American Military Experience in the Mexican War* (College Station: Texas A & M University Press, 2000), p. 90.

6. Eisenhower, pp. 73–74.

7. Ibid., p. 80.

8. Ibid., pp. 83–85.

9. T. Harry Williams, *The History of American Wars From 1745 to 1918* (Baton Rouge: Louisiana State University Press, 1981), p. 170.

10. Eisenhower, p. 98–100.

11. Ibid., pp. 100–112.

12. Ibid., pp. 113, 120.

Chapter 4. From Missouri to California

1. Alan Brinkley, *American History: A Survey*, 10th ed. (Boston: McGraw-Hill College, 1999), pp. 19, 438, 558.

2. John M. Murrin et al., *Liberty, Equality, Power: A History of the American People* (Forth Worth, Tex.: Harcourt Brace College Publishers, 1999), pp. 437–438.

3. Ibid., p. 438.

4. John S. D. Eisenhower, *So Far From God: The U.S. War with Mexico, 1846–1848* (New York: Random House, 1989), pp. 200–203.

5. Ibid., pp. 213–214.

6. Ibid., pp. 224–226.

7. Ibid., pp. 226–229.

Chapter 5. From Monterrey to Buena Vista

1. T. Harry Williams, *The History of American Wars from 1745 to 1918* (New York: Alfred A. Knopf, 1981), p. 172.

2. John S. D. Eisenhower, *So Far From God: The U.S. War with Mexico, 1846–1848* (New York: Random House, 1989), pp. 132–133.

3. Ibid., pp. 135–137.

4. Ibid., p. 138.

5. Ibid., p. 139.

6. Ibid., p. 140.

7. Ibid., pp. 143, 149.

8. Ruth R. Olivera and Liliance Crete, *Life in Mexico Under Santa Anna, 1822–1855* (Norman: University of Oklahoma Press, 1991), pp. 29–30.

9. Eisenhower, p. 187.

Chapter 6. Doniphan's Epic March

1. John S. D. Eisenhower, *So Far From God: The U.S. War with Mexico, 1846–1848* (New York: Random House, 1989), pp. 242–243.

2. Ibid., p. 233.

3. Ibid., pp. 246–247.

4. Ibid., p. 250.

Chapter 7. From Veracruz to Puebla

1. Timothy D. Johnson, *Winfield Scott: The Quest for Military Glory* (Lawrence: University Press of Kansas, 1998), p. 227.

2. Ibid., pp. 2, 153.

3. Mark Crawford, ed., *Encyclopedia of the Mexican-American War* (Santa Barbara, Calif.: ABC-CLIO, 1999), p. 261.

4. John S. D. Eisenhower, *So Far From God: The U.S. War with Mexico, 1846–1848* (New York: Random House, 1989), p. 269.

5. Crawford, p. 20.

6. Eisenhower, pp. 278–279.

7. Ibid., pp. 279–283, 295.

8. Crawford, pp. 71–73.

9. Eisenhower, pp. 269, 296.

10. Ibid., pp. 298, 302, 306.

Chapter 8. From Puebla to Mexico City

1. John S. D. Eisenhower, *So Far From God: The U.S. War with Mexico, 1846–1848* (New York: Random House, 1989), pp. 319–321.

2. Edward H. Moseley and Paul C. Clark, Jr., *Historical Dictionary of the United States–Mexican War* (Lanham, Md.: Scarecrow Press, 1997), p. 88.

3. Eisenhower, p. 325.

4. Ibid., p. 327.

5. Ibid., pp. 332–338.

6. Ibid., pp. 337–339.

7. Ibid., pp. 338–342.

Chapter 9. Making Peace

1. John S. D. Eisenhower, *So Far From God: The U.S. War with Mexico, 1846–1848* (New York: Random House, 1989), pp. 305–307.

2. Edward H. Moseley and Paul C. Clark, Jr., *Historical Dictionary of the United States–Mexican War* (Lanham, Md.: Scarecrow Press, 1997), p. 195.

3. Eisenhower, pp. 360–361.

4. Ibid., pp. 366–367.

Chapter 10. How the War Affected Mexico

1. Alan Brinkley, *American History: A Survey,* 10th ed. (Boston: McGraw-Hill College, 1999), p. 19.

2. Ibid., pp. 442, 558–560.

3. Ruth R. Olivera and Liliance Crete, *Life in Mexico Under Santa Anna, 1822–1855* (Norman: University of Oklahoma Press, 1991), p. 174.

4. Edward H. Moseley and Paul C. Clark, Jr., *Historical Dictionary of the United States–Mexican War* (Lanham, Md.: Scarecrow Press, 1997), pp. 71–72.

5. Michael C. Meyer, *The Course of Mexican History* (New York: Oxford University Press, 1979), p. 352; Howard F. Cline, *The United States and Mexico* (Cambridge, Mass.: Harvard University Press, 1965), p. 313.

6. Meyer, pp. 373–380.

7. Ibid., pp. 381–401.

8. Charles C. Cumberland, *Mexico: The Struggle for Modernity* (New York: Oxford University Press, 1968), p. 211.

9. John M. Murrin et al., *Liberty, Equality, Power: A History of the American People,* 2nd ed. (Fort Worth, Tex.: Harcourt Brace College, 1999), pp. 758–759.

10. Cline, pp. 313–314.

Chapter 11. How the War Affected the United States

1. Edward H. Moseley and Paul C. Clark, Jr., *Historical Dictionary of the United States–Mexican War* (Lanham, Md.: Scarecrow Press, 1997), p. 279.

Further Reading

Books

Carter, Alden R. *The Mexican War: Manifest Destiny.* Danbury, Conn.: Franklin Watts Incorporated, 1992.

Jacobs, William J. *War With Mexico.* Brookfield, Conn.; Millbrook Press, Incorporated, 1993.

Kent, Zachary. *Zachary Taylor.* Danbury, Conn.: Children's Press, 1988.

Lawson, Don. *The United States in the Mexican War.* New York: HarperCollins Children's Book Group, 1988.

Nardo, Don. *The Mexican-American War.* San Diego: Lucent Books, 1991.

Internet Addresses

Aztec Club of 1847. *Military Society of the Mexican War.* © 2001. <http://www.aztecclub.com/nav1.htm>.

Lee, Roger A. "The Mexican-American War." *The History Guy.* © 1998–2000. <http://www.historyguy.com/Mexican-American_War.html>.

The Mexican-American War Memorial Homepage. n.d. <http://sunsite.unam.mx/revistas/1847/>.

Index